Britain and Suez
The lion's last roar

The Suez War of 1956 marked the end of the British Empire, with the Government of Anthony Eden forced into a humiliating ceasefire as it tried to seize the Suez Canal and overthrow the Egyptian government. For almost forty years historians have tried to understand the causes of the war and the reasons for British failure.

The Lion's Last War is the first textbook to combine key documents with a concise analysis of events. Scott Lucas introduces readers to the personalities involved, assessing their strengths and weaknesses. He considers the intrigue between Britain, France, and Israel to attack Egypt, uncovering the secret role of agencies like MI6, Britain's foreign intelligence service, and pointing to the 'regional' influence of countries like Syria, Jordan and Iraq. Most importantly, Dr Lucas re-examines the Anglo-American alliance and its disintegration during Suez.

Scott Lucas is Lecturer in Modern History at the University of Birmingham

Documents in Contemporary History is a series designed for sixth-formers and undergraduates in higher education: it aims to provide both an overview of specialist research on topics in post-1939 British history and a wide-raning selection of primary source material.

Already published

Alan Booth *British economic development since 1945*

Stephen Brooke *Reform and reconstruction: Britain after the war, 1945–51*

Kevin Jefferys *War and reform: British politics during the Second World War*

Scott Lucas *Britain and Suez: The lion's last roar*

Ritchie Ovendale *British defence policy since 1945*

Forthcoming

Stuart Ball *The Convervative Party, 1940–1992*

John Bayliss *Anglo-American relations: the rise and fall of the special relationship*

Steven Fielding *The Labour Party since 1951*

Sean Greenwood *Britain and the European integration since the Second World War*

Harriet Jones *The politics of affluence, Britain 1951–64*

Jane Lewis *Women in post-war British society*

Rodney Lowe *Britain's post-war welfare state*

Panikos Panayi *The impact of immigration*

Harold L. Smith *Britain in the Second World War: a social history*

Sabine Wichert *The integrity of their quarrel: Northern Ireland, 1939 to present day*

Chris Wrigley *British trade unions since 1945*

Documents in Contemporary History

Britain and Suez
The lion's last roar

Edited by
Scott Lucas
Lecturer in Modern History, University of Birmingham

Manchester University Press
Manchester and New York
Distributed exclusively in the USA and Canada by St. Martin's Press

Published by Manchester University Press
Oxford Road, Manchester M13 9NR, UK
and Room 400, 175 Fifth Avenue, New York, NY 10010, USA

Distributed exclusively in the USA and Canada
by St. Martin's Press, Inc., 175 Fifth Avenue, New York,
NY 10010, USA

British Library Cataloguing-in-Publication Data
A catalogue record for this book is available from the British Library

Library of Congress Cataloguing-in-Publication Data
Lucas, Scott.
    Britain and Suez : The lion's last roar / by Scott Lucas.
        p.   cm. — (Documents in contemporary history)
    Includes bibliographical references (p.   ).
    ISBN 0–7190–4579–7. — ISBN 0–7190–4580–0 (pbk. : alk. paper)
    1. Egypt—History—Intervention, 1956. 2. Great Britain—Foreign
relations—1945–   I. Title. II. Series.
DT107.83.L835   1996
962.05′3—dc20   95–23335
                                                          CIP

ISBN 0 7190 4579 7 *hardback*
      0 7190 4580 0 *paperback*

First published 1996

99 98 97 96 95   10 9 8 7 6 5 4 3 2 1

Typeset in Great Britain by Servis Filmsetting Ltd, Manchester
Printed in Great Britain by Bell & Bain Ltd, Glasgow

To my grandparents

Contents

Acknowledgements

I am grateful to all those who helped me with the preparation of this book. The series editor, Kevin Jefferys, and Jane Thorniley-Walker of Manchester University Press advised me on the structure of the text, while Juliet Smith of the University of Birmingham lent a student's view of the content. As always, Helen Laville provided invaluable counsel at critical times.

I am especially thankful to the students, past and present, of my Suez seminar at the University of Birmingham. Their enthusiasm has revived my interest in the topic, and their insight and argument has reminded me that the story of Suez is never complete.

I would like to thank the following for the use of extracts from documents and texts:

Public Record Office (2.1, 2.5, 2.8, 3.3, 3.5, 3.9, 5.3, 6.2, 7.1, 7.12, 7.13, 7.14, 7.15, 8.1, 8.2, 8.3, 8.4, 8.11, 8.13, 8.14, 9.2, 9.3, 9.4, 10.2, 10.4, 10.5, 11.2, 11.4, 11.5, 11.6, 12.3, 12.8, 12.9, 12.10, 12.15, 12.18, 12.19, 13.1, 13.2, 13.4, 13.5, 13.9, 14.2); Trustees of the Avon Papers (3.4, 13.11, 13.14); Weidenfeld and Nicolson (2.12, 3.6, 4.2, 4.3); Constable and Company, Limited (3.8, 10.1, 11.1).

The cover photograph of Anthony Eden is reprinted courtesy of the Trustees of the Avon Papers and the University Library at the University of Birmingham.

Chronology of events

1869
Completion of Suez Canal to link Mediterranean with Red Sea.

1876
Purchase of forty-four per cent of shares in Suez Canal Company by British Government.

1882
Occupation of Egypt by British troops.

1914
Egypt declared a protectorate of the British Empire.

1915
Sykes–Picot Agreement divides Middle East into British and French spheres of influence.

1920
League of Nations awards Britain the mandates for Iraq, Transjordan, and Palestine.

1922
Egypt granted independence by Britain.

1930
Anglo-Iraqi Treaty grants independence to Iraq and British operation of military bases in the country.

1936
Anglo-Egyptian Treaty ends British occupation of cities like
Alexandria and Cairo but confirms British operation of Suez
Canal Base.

1946
Failure to revise Anglo-Egyptian Treaty because of dispute over
the future of the Anglo-Egyptian Sudan.

1948
Creation of state of Israel.

1948–49
First Arab–Israeli War.

1950
25 May   Issurance of Tripartite Declaration by Britain,
France, and the US to prevent aggression between
Israel and Arab States and to regulate arms
shipments to the Middle East.

1951
8 October   Abrogation by Egypt of 1936 Anglo-Egyptian
Treaty.

1952
July   Egyptian Revolution: King Farouk abdicates and
military junta takes power.

1953
20 January   Inauguration of Dwight Eisenhower as President
of the United States.

1954
March   Gamal Abdel Nasser becomes President of Egypt.
19 October   Signature of new Anglo-Egyptian Treaty: British
troops to leave Suez Canal Base by June 1956
although they may re-enter during war or threat
of war.

| December | Agreement by Britain and the United States to seek an Arab–Israeli settlement through Operation ALPHA. |

1955

20 February	Meeting between Anthony Eden and Gamal Abdel Nasser in Cairo.
24 February	Signature of defence pact between Turkey and Iraq.
28 February	Israeli raid upon Egyptian town of Gaza.
4 April	British accession to the Turkish–Iraqi defence pact, renamed the Baghdad Pact.
5 April	Anthony Eden succeeds Winston Churchill as British Prime Minister.
27 September	President Nasser announces Egyptian purchase of arms from the Soviet bloc.
December	Britain and the United States agree to fund the construction of the High Aswan Dam in Egypt.

1956

30 January	Start of summit in Washington between Prime Minister Eden and President Eisenhower.
March	Operation ALPHA collapses after failure of mission by American envoy Robert Anderson.
28 March	United States agrees to join Britain in Operation OMEGA, a long-term programme to isolate Nasser in the Middle East.
19 July	US Secretary of State Dulles withdraws the offer of funding for the High Aswan Dam.
26 July	President Nasser announces nationalisation of the Suez Canal Company.
10 August	Britain's 'War Cabinet', the Egypt Committee, approves Operation MUSKETEER, an Anglo-French military plan to occupy Egyptian cities and remove President Nasser from power.
16–23 August	First London Conference of Maritime Nations to seek an international solution for the Suez Canal.
3 September	Start of Menzies mission to Cairo.
10 September	Egypt Committee accepts American proposal for a Suez Canal Users Association.

10 September	Egypt Committee approves Operation MUSKETEER REVISE, a military plan to overthrow President Nasser through bombing and psychological warfare and to occupy the Suez Canal Zone.
19 September	Start of Second London Conference of Maritime Nations to discuss Suez Canal Users Association.
5 October	Start of talks at the United Nations on the Suez Crisis.
12 October	Acceptance by the United Nations Security Council of Six Principles to govern the operation of the Suez Canal.
14 October (1:30 p.m.)	Prime Minister Eden proposes further negotiations with Egypt in Geneva.
14 October (3:00 p.m.)	Prime Minister Eden meets two French envoys and agrees to discuss Anglo-French-Israeli operation against Egypt.
22 October	First talks between high-ranking British, French, and Israeli officials at Sèvres in France.
24 October	Second talks at Sèvres; agreement in Sèvres Protocol for an Israeli attack upon Egypt, followed by Anglo-French bombing of Egypt and occupation of the Suez Canal Zone.
29 October	Start of Israeli attack upon Egypt.
30 October	Issuance of Anglo-French 'ultimatum' to Egypt and Israel.
31 October	Start of Anglo-French bombing of Egypt.
5 November	Anglo-French paratroop drop to take Port Said and Port Faud at the northern end of the Suez Canal.
6 November (dawn)	Main landing of Anglo-French land force in Suez Canal Zone.
6 November (9:45 a.m.)	British Cabinet agrees to stop military operations at midnight.
3 December	Foreign Secretary Lloyd announces that British troops will be withdrawn from the Suez Canal Zone.

1957

10 January	Harold Macmillan succeeds Anthony Eden as Prime Minister.

Introduction: The telling of the tale

The history of Britain's role in the Suez War has developed in three phases. The first was to establish what happened. Although a war is an obvious event, Suez was no ordinary war. Did British soldiers enter the Suez Canal Zone in November 1956 as part of an attack with France and Israel against Egypt or were they peacekeepers, separating Egyptian and Israeli forces?

Within a year of the war, French authors Merry and Serge Bromberger claimed that the British Prime Minister, Anthony Eden, arranged top-secret meetings with French and Israeli officials. Through this collusion, the three countries soon agreed a co-ordinated assault to occupy the Canal Zone and then strike at Egyptian cities. The British Government, now led by Harold Macmillan, maintained its silence, but other historians put the story together from confidential sources. The Canadian writer Terence Robertson gave a partial account of the collusion, and in 1966 the first British versions appeared. Relying heavily on interviews with Ministers from the Eden Government, Hugh Thomas detailed how Foreign Secretary Selwyn Lloyd travelled to France to negotiate the agreement for collusion, the Sèvres Protocol. Peter Calvocoressi, researching the BBC television series *Suez: Ten Years On*, received the first on-the-record account from Christian Pineau, the French Foreign Minister during Suez; and Anthony Nutting, the former Minister of State in the British Foreign Office, published the comprehensive account by a British participant the following year.

It is a tribute to, or a criticism of, the tenacity of official history that Eden and his advisers publicly denied collusion for more than twenty years. Eden, later Lord Avon, maintained until his death in 1977 that he was only trying to preserve peace in the Middle East and Lloyd's

1

account, published in 1978, devoted an entire chapter to a convoluted argument that the meetings with the French and Israelis did not constitute a secret agreement to attack Egypt. However, further revelations filled in the details, with Pineau contributing a book and Israeli Prime Minister David Ben-Gurion authorising publication of the Sèvres Protocol. Thus, history moved to a second phase, the attribution of responsibility for Britain's failure at Suez.

The debate revolved around Eden. In 1958, Winston Churchill's son Randolph, a London journalist, had published a book-length denunciation of the former Prime Minister, and French officials had reinforced the criticisms with private information to authors like the Brombergers. However, it was Eden's own memoirs in 1960 which fuelled the argument with his diligent but largely unsuccessful attempt to clear himself of any blame. From that point, most reviews of Suez returned to the question of Eden's motives. Critics accused Eden of delusions of grandeur, short-sightedness, or weakness in temperament. Defenders did not deny collusion but argued that co-operation with France and Israel was justified or that factors beyond Eden's control, such as the pressure of the crisis or his poor health, contributed to the ill-fated decision. Even comprehensive accounts were constrained by the central role of Eden – Nutting, for example, concludes his memoirs with bitter criticism of his former friend. The process culminated in the 1980s with two contrasting biographies of Eden. David Carlton castigated the Prime Minister for his inept handling of the crisis and obsession with vanquishing the Egyptian leader, Gamal Abdel Nasser, while Robert Rhodes James portrayed Eden as a courageous and able Prime Minister despite the mistakes of Suez.

Yet Eden, while personalising the debate on his leadership, also broadened the context of that discussion. In his quest for vindication, he blamed others such as the French, other British politicians, and, above all, the Americans for undermining his position. Even if the charges were wayward, participants in Suez were forced to respond and historians obligated to note the exchanges. For example, US President Dwight Eisenhower went to great lengths in his own memoirs to defend his Administration against Eden's allegation of betrayal, while the earliest history of American involvement in the crisis, Herman Finer's *Dulles Over Suez*, supported Eden's argument with a lengthy indictment of the American Secretary of State, John Foster Dulles.

The study of Washington's role in the conflict soon became part of a broader question of whether Eisenhower or Foster Dulles controlled foreign policy. The memoir devoting the greatest attention to the crisis, Emmet Hughes's *The Ordeal of Power*, portrayed Eisenhower as a well-meaning but ill-prepared leader; the President's Chief of Staff, Sherman Adams, tried to correct the image but with little insight into Suez. Instead, it was Townsend Hoopes's study *The Devil and John Foster Dulles*, that crystallised the common perception of a President leaving responsibility for foreign policy to a strong-willed, anti-Communist Secretary of State. Inevitably, there was a reaction against this portrayal. Defenders of Eisenhower discovered a skilful President who supervised foreign policy while delegating its implementation to officials like Foster Dulles. Stephen Ambrose's *Eisenhower the President*, published in 1982, became a model for later works with its praise for a shrewd leader who was at his best in a crisis.

The third phase of the history slowly emerged amidst these general arguments. Instead of focusing upon the responsibility of particular individuals, some authors began to look for broader reasons why decisions were taken and why those policies succeeded or failed. The approach was foreshadowed in a study of the Anglo-American relationship by the political scientist Richard Neustadt. The actions of Eden or Foster Dulles may have contributed to the crisis but so did breakdowns in communication, misperceptions, and differences in objectives. Other works, in a less formal manner, put foreign policy in the context of Middle Eastern events. Nutting's *No End of a Lesson*, despite its concentration upon Eden, noted that the actions of the British Government turned not only upon the perceived Egyptian threat but also the long-term strategy of the British alliance with Iraq and Jordan. American journalist Kennett Love, in a 1970 study which is still among the most informative, captured the complexity of Britain's relations with Egypt, while Donald Neff in 1981 published the first comprehensive account of American involvement in the crisis.

Subsequent historians have developed these complexities of Suez by studying aspects of the crisis. Roy Fullick and Geoffrey Powell have surveyed the development of British military operations, Diane Kunz and Lewis Johnman have examined the effect of Britain's economic weakness and dependence upon American finance, and David Devereaux has placed Suez in the context of Britain's strategic planning. On the American side, US relations with Egypt have been examined by Geoffrey Aronson, and its Middle Eastern strategy has been evaluated by H. W. Brands, Ayesha Jalal, and Douglas Little. While advances in French scholarship have been limited, notably by the refusal or delay in releasing Government documents, Israeli authors have produced valuable studies of diplomatic and military strategy, and Mohammed Sayed-Ahmed has added the first scholarly account in English from an Egyptian perspective.

The application of the British thirty-year rule, releasing most Government papers in 1987, and the continued declassification of American memoranda under the Freedom of Information Act, have offered even more opportunities for analysis. With the significant exception of those documents withheld because of 'national security', the raw material for research is in the public domain. Yet it is questionable if historians have taken full advantage of the new material. The two major British biographies of recent years, Rhodes James's *Anthony Eden* and Alistair Horne's *Harold Macmillan*, both made little use of the documents, as Rhodes James published in 1986 and Horne preferred to rely on Macmillan's diary. Among American authors, Peter Hahn has produced a careful analysis of the triangular relationship between Britain, the US, and Egypt, but Stephen Freiberger's *Dawn Over Suez* reduces the crisis to another case of America trying to take over the British position in the Middle East.

In 1991, two contrasting academic studies were published in Britain, Keith Kyle's *Suez* and my own *Divided We Stand: Britain, the US and the Suez Crisis*. Kyle's 656-page account is an ambitious attempt to rewrite the Suez history but relies almost exclusively on British documents. It is also confusing in its analysis, reverting in the end to the image of Eden as valiant but flawed. My shorter book, together with several articles, tried to place British policymaking in a context beyond the Prime Minister. It studied other groups like the Cabinet, the Foreign Office, and the intelligence services and evaluates the Anglo-American relationship against the backdrop of Middle Eastern politics and the influence of countries like France. Many of these arguments are reproduced in this book and in the new edition of *Divided We Stand*, published in paperback in 1996.

So where are we now, almost forty years after the Suez War? Far from being complete, history is only beginning to capture the intricacies behind an event that symbolised the end of Britain's global influence. Contrary to the claims of learned observers, more material is waiting to be discovered, notably:

1 The files of the intelligence services, whose role in Suez has been ignored or underrated by almost all historians. Even if British plans to assassinate Egyptian leaders were more fantasy than reality, there was a sustained British and American effort to overthrow the Cairo regime. The files of MI6, Britain's foreign intelligence service, may be jealously guarded under this country's curious notion of 'freedom of information', but those of the CIA, its American counterpart, are gradually being declassified.

2 The records of treasury departments and financial institutions. Most historians acknowledge that the weakness of the pound hindered Britain's military operations and that American pressure may have forced the British to halt the war. Yet the recent work of Kunz and Johnman is the first to address the issue in detail, and they rely upon documents from the British Exchequer. Sources like the Bank of England and the US Treasury remain unexplored.

3 Documents on special military operations, notably psychological warfare. The final British plan was not a conventional assault but sustained bombing and propaganda to encourage the Egyptian people to overthrow President Nasser. It was only after that scheme failed that British troops landed in the Canal Zone, but many historians have ignored the unique if flawed psychological strategy.

4 Information from countries other than Britain and the United States. Many of the important questions in Suez – for example, the nature of the collusion against Egypt – may be answered from these sources, but restrictions continue to frustrate historians. Apart from some papers in its Foreign Office, which played only a small role in the crisis, the records of the French Government are closed, and key material in many Israeli archives only available to a small number of researchers. Few, if any, documents are available in Arab countries. It is unclear if the situation will improve, but some authors, notably in Israel, are making new discoveries despite the limitations.

All this promises further revelations in the Suez story; however, there is no need for historians to scurry like squirrels for the latest nut to fall from the archives. Instead, a fresh look at available documents should address outstanding questions, including:

1 Why did the United States and Britain co-operate on some issues in the Middle East but disagree on others? For example, the two countries had agreed in March 1956 to remove Nasser from power, yet the Americans refused to support a British invasion that might have achieved that goal.

2 To what extent was Anthony Eden in control of British policy? Some authors have considered whether advice from Harold Macmillan, then Chancellor of the Exchequer, may have pushed Eden into the attack on Egypt, but the situation may be far more complex. Government agencies like MI6 not only pressed for the overthrow of Nasser but had links with Israel long before collusion was considered.

3 How did relations within the Middle East affect the course of the crisis? Even the Arab–Israeli conflict, a key part of the story, has been treated briefly by many historians, and rivalries among Arab states, notably Egypt and Iraq, have received even less attention. Yet Britain's need to maintain its Middle Eastern position through partnership with Arab countries and the United States' links with Saudi Arabia indicate that Suez cannot be separated from the regional dimension.

4 Was the Suez War inevitable? In most of the literature, the conflict is treated as a foregone conclusion, yet there is strong evidence that, two weeks before the war, Eden had called off the military operation and was preparing to negotiate with Egypt over control of the Suez Canal. History would have been rewritten: Eden could have been hailed as a peacemaker or criticised for his retreat from a showdown, but Britain could have maintained some semblance of influence and the Anglo-American 'alliance' would have worked, if only to restrain London.

5 Why did collusion occur? The centrepiece of the Suez tale is unexplained with historians assuming that Britain, France, and Israel had a common interest in attacking Egypt. This common interest, however, had not brought the three countries together before October 1956 and there were obvious disadvantages if the plot was exposed. Thus, the question remains: what could have compelled Anthony Eden, six hours after halting military preparations for war with Egypt, to accept the French offer of talks with the Israelis?

1

Background

The roots of the Suez Crisis lay in British interests in the Middle East dating from the mid-nineteenth century. By 1945, these interests were challenged by pressure for an independent state of Israel, the emergence of the US as an influential power, and the replacement in Arab countries of 'old guard' elites, often supported by Britain, with younger regimes which proclaimed nationalist agendas. Geographically, the centre of the evolving conflict was the Suez Canal, completed in 1869 between the Mediterranean Ocean and the Red Sea. Bisecting Egypt from north to south, the Canal allowed ships to move from Europe to India and the Far East without the long voyage around the southern end of Africa. Its control by France and Britain was an important symbol of the continuing dominance of those countries in the region.

In 1876, the Egyptian leader, the Khedive Ismail, sold his forty-four per cent stake in the Paris-based Suez Canal Company to the British Government. Six years later, the Government of William Gladstone reluctantly dispatched troops to Egypt to safeguard the investment, a temporary occupation which would last almost seventy-five years. During World War I, Egypt even became a British protectorate. Although it was granted nominal independence in 1922, the British military remained in cities like Alexandria and Cairo until a 1936 treaty formally established Britain's long-term position within the Suez Canal Zone. During World War II, the Canal Zone Base was the largest in the world, supplying troops and equipment for the Middle East, North Africa, and Europe.

With the dissolution of the Ottoman Empire after World War I, the British position in Egypt became the pivot of its power in the Middle East. The Sykes–Picot agreement with France divided the region into spheres of influence, and Britain confirmed its ties with the local elite by recognising Sharif Hussein of Mecca as the ruler of the Arabian Peninsula and placing his sons, Feisal and Abdullah, on the thrones of the British mandates of Iraq and Jordan. Britain even ensured, in the final peace settlement and the negotiations of the new League of Nations, that it received the mandate for

Palestine. Only Saudi Arabia, where King Ibn Saud ousted Sharif Hussein in 1926, escaped British or French oversight.

These high-level ties were supported by a network of political and economic arrangements. Although Iraq was granted independence in 1930, the subsequent Anglo-Iraqi Treaty guaranteed British rights to military bases until 1957, and British diplomats worked closely with Iraqi Prime Minister Nuri Sa'id, who was even more influential than the King. In Jordan, King Abdullah was carefully advised by Sir Alec Kirkbride. British banks and businesses dominated foreign investment, and access to oil was guaranteed by a controlling stake in the Anglo-Iranian Oil Company and a 37.5 per cent share of the Iraqi Petroleum Company.

During World War II, Britain consolidated its position. Fearful of leaders who might back Germany, British officials sponsored a coup in Iraq, replaced the Shah of Iran with his son, and surrounded the Egyptian Palace with tanks to force the King to replace his Prime Minister with a more 'suitable' leader. The military stand at El Alamein in western Egypt checked the German advance, but the lesser-known British defeat of Vichy French forces in Syria and the Lebanon was just as significant for the future of the Middle East.

Yet, if Britain won the war, it could not overcome peacetime problems, of which the future of the Arabs and Jews in Palestine was only the most prominent example. The new Labour Government of Clement Attlee, recognising that resentment among Arab nationalists of foreign 'domination' was increasing, trumpeted a policy of 'partnership' in which London would finance the economic development of the region. Hopes for this were soon dashed, however. With a quarter to a third of its assets depleted by the war, Britain could not afford to maintain existing commitments, let alone extend more economic aid. The strain hastened departure from the Indian subcontinent, Greece, and Palestine, and severe financial crises in 1947 and 1949 killed off any hope of British revival. Politically, the revision of the 1936 Anglo-Egyptian Treaty collapsed over a dispute about control of the Sudan, and the 1948 Anglo-Iraqi Treaty was abandoned after violent demonstrations in Baghdad. Only in newly independent Jordan was a new agreement completed.

The predicament was complicated by the evolution of American policy. The emergence of American interest in the region could be a lifeline to Britain with joint military planning and economic aid from Washington, but the US concern with particular cases, notably the fate of the Jews in Palestine and oil production in Saudi Arabia, was more often a hindrance than a contribution to Anglo-American co-operation. The expansion of the Cold War and the aftermath of the 1948-49 Arab–Israeli war finally yielded agreements in principle – notably the 1950 Tripartite Declaration in which Britain, the United States and France promised to control arms sales and prevent aggression in the Middle East – but the practical effects were limited. With their commitments in Europe and Korea, the Americans would not deploy military forces in the Middle East, and US officials were still wary of British 'colonialism', especially after London threatened war over Iran's nationalisation of the Anglo-Iranian Oil Company in 1951.

Egypt was at the heart of these problems. Desperate to secure its rights to the Suez Canal Base, Britain tried to renew the 1936 Anglo–Egyptian Treaty through a proposal for a Middle Eastern Command including France and the United States. The effort was futile, since Egypt unilaterally abandoned the 1936 Treaty days before it was asked to join the Middle Eastern Command. Talks for a Middle Eastern defence system dragged on until June 1953, but the Egyptians never accepted Western control of the Canal Base. Instead, British troops faced persistent attacks from a population committed to their removal from Egyptian soil.

Events increasingly isolated the British and brought Washington into the centre of affairs. When rioters in Cairo in January 1952 burned British-owned buildings and killed eight Europeans and Canadians, only the efforts of the US Ambassador prevented Egypt from breaking diplomatic relations with Britain. Six months later, Egypt's King Farouk was overthrown by a group led by Free Officers in the military. The *coup* was sudden but far from a surprise to the Americans; six of the Free Officers had studied in the US, and American officials had been in contact with the key plotters, including an army colonel named Nasser, since October 1951. While the British panicked, the US Embassy established close links with the new regime.

More orthodox changes of government raised further questions for the Anglo-American alliance. The 1951 election of the Conservative Party in Britain, with the return of Winston Churchill as Prime Minister, posed no problem since Churchill's aspiration for a return of British imperial glory was still based on a special relationship with the US. The inauguration of Churchill's wartime colleague, Dwight Eisenhower, as US President in January 1953 was a different matter. Eisenhower's insistence that 'the two strongest Western powers must not appear before the world as a combination of forces to compel adherence to the status quo'[1] was bolstered by a Secretary of State, John Foster Dulles, who believed that only American leadership could guarantee the peace and security of the Free World against Soviet Communism. After a Middle Eastern tour in May 1953, Foster Dulles was convinced that American support of British proposals for Middle Eastern defence was useless. Given the Egyptians' 'intense distrust and dislike for the British', the troops in the Suez Canal Base were 'more a factor of instability than stability'.[2] The US would have to act unilaterally, mediating an Anglo-Egyptian settlement and then developing a 'Northern

[1] Public Record Office, PREM11/486, Eisenhower to Churchill, 16 March 1953.
[2] *Foreign Relations of the United States*, 1952–54, vol. IX, p. 379.

Tier' defence system of Turkey, Pakistan, and Iran on the southern border of the Soviet Union.

American support for Britain as the dominant Western power in the Middle East was no longer assured. Yet an 'alliance' might be maintained, provided the interests of both countries were satisfied. Thus, in August 1953, the Eisenhower Administration's fears of a Communist takeover of Iran allowed the CIA to work with the British foreign intelligence service, MI6, to overthrow the Mossadegh Government which had nationalised the Anglo-Iranian Oil Company. Britain not only accepted US military aid to Iraq and Pakistan and American sponsorship of a Turkish–Pakistani defence pact but also, under pressure from the US, concluded a new Anglo-Egyptian Treaty in October 1954. British troops would leave the Canal Zone by June 1956; however, they could re-enter the Base in the event of war or threat of war. Building on these successes, Washington and London agreed in November 1954 on a plan to solve the toughest problem, the dispute between the Arab States and Israel. The top-secret project was code-named ALPHA.

2

Seeds of conflict

On 20 February 1955 in Cairo, British Foreign Secretary Anthony Eden met his future enemy, Egyptian President Gamal Abdel Nasser, for the first and only time. Eden later wrote in his memoirs of Nasser's shiftiness and insincerity, but his report at the time was much more favourable.

2.1   *1955   21 February*
Letter from Eden to Prime Minister Winston Churchill

I was impressed by Nasser, who seemed forthright and friendly although not open to conviction on the Turkish–Iraqi business [the Turkish–Iraqi defence pact mentioned in the following paragraph]. No doubt jealousy plays a part in this, and a frustrated desire to lead the Arab world.

Public Record Office, FO371/1 ₁5492/V1073/289, Cairo to Foreign Office, Cable 269

Why then did relations deteriorate between the two countries with Eden seeing Nasser as the source of all evil in the Middle East? The answer lies in other events.

Four days after the Eden–Nasser meeting, Turkey and Iraq signed a pact in which each country would defend the other against outside attack. Initially, the British Foreign Office was surprised by the Turkish and Iraqi intentions but, with the Anglo-Iraqi Treaty due to expire in 1957, Eden and his officials soon swung behind the plan. On 4 April, Britain joined the Turkish–Iraqi arrangement, converting it into the Baghdad Pact.

11

2.2   1955   4 April
Special Agreement between the Government of the United Kingdom and the Government of Iraq

The Government of the United Kingdom of Great Britain and Northern Ireland and the Government of the Kingdom of Iraq, considering that the United Kingdom intends to accede to the Pact of Mutual Co-operation between Iraq and Turkey signed at Bagdad on February 24, 1955, ... have agreed as follows:

Article 1
The two Contracting Governments shall maintain and develop peace and friendship between their two countries and shall co-operate for their security and defence in accordance with the Pact of Mutual Co-operation. ...

Article 5
In accordance with Article 1 of the Pact, there shall be close co-operation between the competent authorities of the two Governments for the defence of Iraq. This co-operation shall include planning, combined training and the provision of such facilities as may be agreed upon between the two Contracting Governments for this purpose and with the object of maintaining Iraq's armed forces at all times in a state of efficiency and readiness.

Documents on International Affairs, 1955, pp. 293–4

Eight days after the Eden-Nasser meeting, two Israeli platoons attacked pumping installations and army buildings inside the Gaza Strip, killing thirty-eight Egyptians. Ostensibly, the raid was revenge for Cairo's execution of Israeli spies and the seizure of an Israeli ship defying the Egyptian blockade of the Suez Canal, but it also marked a change in Israeli policy. David Ben-Gurion, the first Prime Minister of Israel, had just returned to the Cabinet as Defence Minister. While the current Prime Minister, Moshe Sharett, sought reconciliation with Egypt, Ben-Gurion and the chief of the Israeli military, Moshe Dayan, believed that Israel must display its military superiority to deter any Arab attacks.[1]

[1] See Shlaim (1983).

2.3   1955   2 March
Speech by Prime Minister Sharett to the Israeli Parliament, the Knesset

Israel has never wanted bloodshed anywhere in the world, and certainly not among her own citizens and neighbours; what is more, I declare that Israel has a strong desire to be a law-abiding State. It should be clear, however, that the armistice between us and Egypt is also a law which must be observed by both sides. The obligation contained in the Armistice Agreement to proceed toward a complete and comprehensive peace settlement is a law which both sides are obliged to observe. If Egypt, in contravention of its international obligations, declares again and again that it maintains and has a right to maintain a state of war against Israel . . ., then Egypt bears responsibility for the results. These results include armed clashes – all the more likely if Egypt deliberately provokes them – and bloody battles which develop. Egypt must choose between the existing situation with all its losses and dangers or absolute abstention from hostile actions, strict observance of the Armistice Agreement and progress toward peace.

Documents on International Affairs, 1955, p. 346

2.4   1955   3 March
Speech by President Nasser

Today, brothers, we live in 1955, and today is different from yesterday. I tell Israel and those who make threats in Israel's name that there is an old saying, 'A man lies and people believe him; he lies again and people still believe him; he lies yet again and begins to believe his own lies.' If Israel thinks that it defeated the Egyptian army in 1948, and, believing this fable, makes threats, then let me tell Israel that we are ready for her. . . .

I tell them that we shall defend the homeland and meet aggression with aggression. The Commander-in-Chief of the Armed Forces has been instructed to answer aggression with aggression. The Commander-in-Chief of the Armed Forces has also been instructed to take action to protect our homeland's borders. All Egypt's potential will be mobilised for this purpose. If we enter the battle today, we shall be able to make up for what happened in the past.

Documents on International Affairs, 1955, pp. 346–7

Together, Gaza and the Baghdad Pact jeopardised any Egyptian accommodation with Britain. The Pact's central member was Iraq, a rival to Egypt for leadership of the Arab world. Britain's solution was the prospect of Egypt joining the Iraqis as the corner-stones of the defence system, but Nasser, perceiving Israel as the chief threat, saw no advantage in a pact directed against the Soviet Union. Progress could only come through an Arab–Israeli settlement which would overcome incidents like the Gaza raid.

Britain and the United States pursued that solution throughout 1955. By May, Nasser agreed to speak with envoys shuttling between Cairo and Tel Aviv, and British and American negotiators drafted a provisional settlement with Israel ceding two 'triangles' of land in the Negev desert to Egypt. However, when the US Ambassador to Egypt, Henry Byroade, tried to talk details with Nasser on 9 June, the Egyptian President linked any negotiations to the question of arms for the Egyptian military.[2] Nasser's anger over Gaza had been reinforced by discovery of French arms shipments to Israel, and he was under pressure from Egyptian army officers to act quickly.

2.5   1955   12 June
Statement by President Nasser to the British Ambassador to Egypt, Sir Ralph Stevenson

I have tried my utmost to obtain from you the arms required for the defence of my country, but I have not been successful. I cannot stand by with folded arms in the face of Israel. I consider what you have said as a threat which I am not prepared to accept. You are free to do whatever you like and I am free to do as I please.

Cited in Public Record Office, FO371/113675/JE1194/190, BBC Monitoring Report, 8 October 1955

In principle, British and American officials were willing to sell some equipment to Egypt, but they faced unexpected obstacles. Eden, now Prime Minister, had turned against Nasser when Egyptian propaganda supported Saudi Arabia in its dispute with Britain over territory on the Arabian peninsula.[3] Eisenhower was more amenable toward Nasser,

---

[2] US National Archives, Department of State, Central File, 780.5/6-955, Cairo to State Department, Cable 1881, 9 June 1955.

[3] Public Record Office, FO371/113608/JE1057/7, de Zulueta minute, 22 June 1955, and subsequent minutes, and JE1057/8, de Zulueta to Graham, 8 July 1955, and subsequent minutes.

authorising an initial sale of $11 million of arms, but Egypt was short of dollars and the US would not give any arms on credit unless American military 'advisers' were also sent to Cairo.[4]

Foster Dulles tried to spur ALPHA with a speech in August, calling for a comprehensive settlement.

2.6 1955 26 August
Speech by Secretary of State Dulles to the Council on Foreign Relations

To end the plight of the 900,000 [Palestinian] refugees requires that these uprooted people should, through resettlement and – to such an extent as may be feasible – repatriation, be enabled to resume a life of dignity and self-respect. To this end, there is need to create more arable land where refugees can find permanent homes and gain their own livelihood through their own work. . . .

The second principal problem which I mentioned is that of fear. The nature of this fear is such that it is hardly within the capacity of the countries of the area, acting alone, to replace the fear with a sense of security. There, as in many other areas, security can be assured only by collective measures which commit decisive power to the deterring of aggression.

President Eisenhower has authorized me to say that, given a solution of the other related problems, he would recommend that the United States join in formal treaty engagements to prevent or thwart any effort by either side to alter by force the boundaries between Israel and its Arab neighbors. I hope that other countries would be willing to join in such a security guaranty, and that it would be sponsored by the United Nations. . . .

If agreement can be reached on these basic problems of refugees, fear, and boundaries, it should prove possible to find solutions for other questions, largely economic, which presently fan the flames of hostility and resentment.

Department of State Bulletin, 5 September 1955, pp. 378–80

However, Nasser had turned to another source for his needs. In June, he had discussed arms sales with Soviet Foreign Minister Dmitri Shepilov. After a renewal of Egyptian–Israeli conflict in the Gaza Strip

---

[4] *Foreign Relations of the United States*, 1955–57, Volume XIV, p. 274.

two months later, the deal was concluded with Egypt receiving 100 tanks and 200 fighters and bombers from the Soviet bloc. Opening an Armed Forces exhibition in Cairo, Nasser announced the arms deal:

2.7   1955   27 September
Speech by President Nasser

We harbour no aggressive intentions; our aims are only peaceful. We want an independent army which will support this country's independent aims. We want a strong army for the purposes of peace, not for those of aggression. I said this in Egypt's name to America, Britain, France, the USSR, Czechoslovakia and many other nations; and then I waited for their replies. What was the result?

From some of these nations I received replies in which they said that they could supply our army with weapons on certain conditions. These conditions I rejected. . . . We may plead and beg for arms and may humiliate ourselves to obtain them, but we shall never abandon our principles; then I waited.

When we received a reply to our request from the Government of Czechoslovakia declaring its readiness to supply us with weapons in accordance with the Egyptian army's needs and on a purely commercial basis, and stating that the transaction would be regarded as any other commercial one, we accepted immediately. . . .

It is with thankfulness that we have accepted this offer, my brothers, for we have in this way accomplished one of the revolution's aims – namely, the creation of a strong national army.

BBC Summary of World Broadcasts, Part IV, 30 September 1955, pp. 17–18

In many books, the arms deal is portrayed as the last straw for Britain and the US, who now saw Nasser as the puppet of Moscow. The reality is far more complex. The British Foreign Secretary, Harold Macmillan, was enraged and his officials noted, 'We may have to get rid of Nasser',[5] but the Americans were reconciled to the turn of events. Special representatives from the State Department and CIA even helped Nasser write the speech, encouraging the Egyptian President to make a gesture of peace to Israel.[6] Although Macmillan, in face-to-face

[5] Public Record Office, FO371/113674/JE1194/152G, Caccia minute, 23 September 1955.
[6] See Lucas (1991, pp. 58–62).

meetings, worked up Foster Dulles' anger, the US Secretary of State finally agreed with his advisers that 'we should not take any threatening or drastic step at this time' because of the 'lack of a better alternative' to Nasser.[7] Macmillan reluctantly fell into line.

2.8   *1955   9 November*
Memorandum by British Foreign Office

We should not write off Egypt or drive her into Russia's arms. There are indications that Nasser does not desire to be identified with the Soviet bloc. It is probable that he envisages a neutralist policy in which the Arab world, with Egypt at its head, would be in a strong bargaining position. . . . We should hope that the next few months will show whether he is ready to mend his fences with the West and avoid further involvement with the Soviet bloc. We should assist him in this period by refraining from any punitive measures, and keeping contact with him over such matters as the Aswan Dam, the Sudan, and other subjects of common interest.

Public Record Office, FO371/113678

2.9   *1955   21 November*
Statement by Secretary of State Dulles to the US National Security Council

Nasser felt that he must hold his job. The Army was the key to holding the job, and the Army was demanding armament. Accordingly, there was no clear demonstration yet that Colonel Nasser actually proposed to turn his back on the West and cast his lot with the Soviet bloc.

Eisenhower Library, Eisenhower Papers, Ann Whitman Series, National Security Meetings, 267th Meeting

> The situation was further complicated because President Eisenhower had suffered a heart attack on 23 September. He was cut off from almost all policymaking until he returned to Washington in early November. Eden, trying to fill the vacuum in Western leadership, launched a series of initiatives; despite his hatred of Nasser, he sought

---

[7] US National Archives, Department of State, Central File, 774.56/10-355, Wilkins memorandum, 3 October 1955.

an accommodation with Egypt and the Soviet Union. His proposal for consultation with Moscow over future arms shipments was rejected by Macmillan and the horrified Americans, and he infuriated the Israelis and again upset Foster Dulles with a sudden attempt to solve the Arab–Israeli question.

2.10   *1955   9 November*
Speech by Prime Minister Eden at the Guildhall

Our one desire is to help to find a means of living which will enable the peoples concerned to dwell side by side in peace. If, for instance, there could be accepted an arrangement between them about their boundaries, we, and I believe the United States, and perhaps other powers also, would be prepared to give a formal guarantee to both sides. This might bring real confidence and security at last. Our countries would also offer substantial help – financial and other – over the tragic problem of the refugees.

Can we not now move even a little further than this? The position today is that the Arabs take their stand on the 1947 and other United Nations resolutions. They have said that they will be willing to discuss terms with Israel on that basis. The Israelis, on the other hand, found themselves on the Armistice Agreement of 1949 and on the present territories which they occupy.

Between these two positions there is, of course, a wide gap, but is it so wide that no negotiation is possible to bridge it?

Documents on International Affairs, 1955, pp. 382–5

Eden only succeeded when he appealed to Eisenhower to proceed quickly with financial assistance for the High Aswan Dam. With the Egyptian population growing faster than its food production, the construction of the Dam was essential for stability and progress. In the wake of the Egyptian–Soviet arms deal, Foster Dulles and Macmillan seized upon the project to win Nasser back to the West. Eden's letter to Eisenhower on 26 November,[8] combining the proposal of aid for the Dam with a request to meet the President and resolve other issues in the Middle East, was quickly followed by agreement with Egypt.

[8] Public Record Office, FO371/113739/JE1423/269G, Foreign Office to Washington, Cable 5631, 26 November 1955.

2.11   *1955   17 December*
Communiqué from the United States, Britain, and Egypt on assistance for construction of the High Aswan Dam

The United States and British Governments assured the Egyptian Government through Mr. Kaissouni [the Egyptian Minister of Finance] of their support in this project, which would be of inestimable importance in the development of the Egyptian economy and in the improvement of the welfare of the Egyptian people. Such assistance would take the form of grants from the United States and the United Kingdom toward defraying foreign exchange costs of the first stages of the work. This phase . . . will take from four to five years. Further, assurance has been given to Mr. Kaissouni that the Governments of the United States and the United Kingdom would, subject to legislative authority, be prepared to consider sympathetically in the light of then existing circumstances further support toward financing the later stages to supplement World Bank financing.

Department of State Bulletin, 26 December 1955, pp. 1050–1

Despite Foster Dulles' reluctance, the President agreed to a meeting in late January so the US could 'show a position of influence' over the British.[9]

The need for the summit was soon apparent. As soon as the Americans approved funding for the Dam, a new crisis emerged. This time, the culprit was Macmillan, who authorised a British attempt to bring Jordan into the Baghdad Pact. Enticed by the British offer of planes and other military equipment, Jordan's King Hussein was receptive. His Ministers hesitated, however, and Saudi Arabia and Egypt, fearing further isolation from their Arab neighbours, financed public demonstrations that threatened to topple the King.[10] Britain's efforts collapsed in humiliation.

2.12   *1955   19 December*
Diary entry of Evelyn Shuckburgh, Assistant Secretary of State in the Foreign Office

Serious rioting in Jordan, and for some reason a very bad day for me which left me utterly depressed about our affairs. I feel we may have

[9] Eisenhower Library, John Foster Dulles Papers, Telephone Calls, White House, Box 10, Eisenhower to Foster Dulles, 28 and 29 November 1955.
[10] See Lucas (1991, pp. 74–6).

'torn Jordan in pieces' as I feared we might. . . . If Saudi/ Egyptian/Communist intrigue can prevent Jordan joining the Pact despite our offers and despite the King and Government wishing to do so, how far the rot has spread!

Evelyn Shuckburgh, *Descent to Suez*, London, 1986, pp. 313–14

Foster Dulles, who had warned Macmillan against the approach to Jordan, was furious and Eisenhower wrote, 'The British never had any sense in the Middle East.'[11]

As Britain was failing in Jordan, the Americans were taking the next and possibly last step with ALPHA. With the Presidential election due in November 1956, there were only a few months of manoeuvre before the 'Jewish vote' became an insuperable obstacle. Robert Anderson, a close friend of Eisenhower, was appointed as envoy for negotiations between Cairo and Tel Aviv. The Foreign Office deferred to the American lead although it was sceptical about the use of a special representative.[12]

Problems such as these had been mitigated by the excellent working relationship between Foster Dulles and Macmillan, but even this was lost in December 1955. Eden, wanting to direct foreign policy, moved the strong-willed Macmillan to the Exchequer and appointed the more modest Selwyn Lloyd as Foreign Secretary.

2.13   *1955   20 December*
Letter from Secretary of State Dulles to Foreign Secretary Macmillan

I am terribly disappointed to learn that the Cabinet shift which you mentioned to me as a possibility has actually occurred. . . . I have come to have great trust and reliance in you and because of this I have looked toward the future with greater confidence.

Eisenhower Library, John Foster Dulles Papers, Subject, Alphabetical, Box 11, Eden–Macmillan–Lloyd Correspondence (2)

---

[11] Eisenhower Library, Eisenhower Papers, Ann Whitman Series, Ann Whitman Diary, Box 7, Eisenhower minute, 16 December 1955.
[12] Public Record Office, FO371/115887/VR1076/504G, Arthur minute, 8 December 1955, and FO371/115887/VR1076/524G, Shuckburgh minute, 16 December 1955.

2.14   *1955   21 December*
Letter from Foreign Secretary Macmillan to Secretary of State Dulles

Just as this country's connexion with America is the most important thing in its foreign relations, so our own personal connexion was at all times in the front of my thinking. I think our work together was useful and good.

Eisenhower Library, John Foster Dulles Papers, Subject, Alphabetical, Box 11, Eden–Macmillan–Lloyd Correspondence (2)

3

Turning against Nasser

Sometimes success comes from adversity rather than prosperity. So Britain, in the midst of political crisis, came close to achieving its goals in the Middle East. The Eden Government had three objectives: to secure the co-operation of the Americans, to build its position around an Iraqi–Jordanian axis, and to curb the threat of Nasser. By the end of March 1956, only weeks after Eden was on the brink of falling from power, all three goals were within grasp.

The turn of events began when Eden arrived in Washington in January 1956 for the summit with Eisenhower. The prospects for the visit were not good, as the Prime Minister was being ridiculed by British newspapers, even those which normally supported the Conservative Party. The campaign was launched by the *Daily Telegraph*:

3.1 *1956 3 January*
Comment in *Daily Telegraph* by Donald Maclachlan

Why are Conservatives around the country restive, and Ministers and backbenchers unenraptured with their leader? There is a favourite gesture of the Prime Minister's which is sometimes recalled to illustrate this sense of disappointment. To emphasise a point, he will clench one fist to smack the open palm of the other hand – but the smack is seldom heard. Most Conservatives, and almost certainly some of the wiser trade union leaders, are waiting to feel the smack of firm Government.

'Waiting for the smack of firm government . . .', *Daily Telegraph*, 3 January 1956, p. 6

The criticism reached such a level that the *Daily Mirror*, which backed the Labour Party, crowed, 'Eden is a FLOP. . . . Even the Tories are

22

saying it now.' The Prime Minister was ill-tempered and jumpy, complaining about the limited time allowed for meeting Eisenhower because of the President's recent heart attack. En route to the US on the *Queen Mary*, he told Foreign Secretary Lloyd, 'I am not going to be treated like this. I will take the next boat home.'[1]

Eden stayed, however, and benefited from a shift in Foster Dulles' attitude toward Nasser. Depressed at difficulties in the initial talks between the Egyptian President and Robert Anderson, the American special envoy, Foster Dulles told Eden, 'Nasser might have become a tool of the Russians.'[2] Although both sides agreed that accommodation with the Egyptians must continue while Anderson was in the Middle East, the Americans now acknowledged that they would seek Britain's co-operation in a programme against Egypt once the talks failed.

3.2   1956   30 January
Foster Dulles to Eden at Washington summit

The Secretary stated that current efforts to find a solution to the Arab–Israeli dispute . . . had not as yet produced any real hopes for an early settlement. It appeared that the Egyptians were dragging their feet. . . . We might soon know whether our whole attitude toward Nasser would have to be changed.

Eisenhower Library, Eisenhower Papers, Ann Whitman Series, International, Box 20, Eden Visit

With the shift in opinion, the Eisenhower Administration viewed Britain's defence of her Middle Eastern position with more sympathy. The two delegations agreed to shows of force, such as the visit of warships to Middle Eastern ports, to uphold the Tripartite Declaration against aggression by Israel or Arab countries. While the US still refused to join the Baghdad Pact, it noted that the grouping served 'the interests of the area as a whole' and backed up the rhetoric with more tanks for Iraq and economic aid for Iran. Foster Dulles even hinted that he would consider the overthrow of the Syrian Government, which supported Nasser and was considered a threat to both Iraq and Jordan. Eden concluded in a cable to his Ministers, 'My personal conviction is that this is the best meeting in Washington we have ever had.'[3]

---

[1] Shuckburgh (1986, p. 327).
[2] Eisenhower Library, Eisenhower Papers, Ann Whitman Series, International, Box 20, Eden Visit, 30 January 1956.
[3] Avon Papers, AP20/24, Washington to Foreign Office, Cable 286, 1 February 1956.

3.3   1956   9 *February*
Statement by Prime Minister Eden to the Cabinet

In the Middle East the most urgent need was to compose the differences between Israel and the Arab States and it had been agreed that the three Governments concerned should reaffirm their intention to carry out the terms of the Tripartite Declaration. . . . American warships were in fact proceeding unobtrusively to take up position in the Eastern Mediterranean and the Red Sea, and British naval forces were conforming with that movement. Agreement had also been reached on means of increasing the effectiveness of [the United Nations] organisation for detecting breaches of the Armistice conditions.

The United States Government had agreed to give their full moral support to the Bagdad Pact, though they were not able to join it. . . .

As regards the [Anglo–Saudi] dispute over Buraimi they had been brought to accept our view that there should be no renewal of arbitration and that progress could best be made by resumption of direct discussions between ourselves and the Saudi. They would support our efforts to prevent this matter from being brought before the Security Council.

Public Record Office, CAB128/30, C.M.10(56)

Eden's elation was short-lived. Back in London, Macmillan was becoming a formidable rival, embarrassing the Prime Minister by forcing the abolition of Government subsidies for bread and milk. The US Embassy observed, 'If the economic outlook improves dramatically, but foreign affairs, which are regarded as Eden's particular province, do not improve, the chances for Macmillan [to become Prime Minister] would be still brighter.'[4]

Humiliation in the Middle East followed. On 1 March, King Hussein dismissed General Glubb, the British commander of Jordan's army, and asked him to leave the country within 24 hours. Britain's entire defence strategy was now in jeopardy.

3.4   1956   1 *March*
Message from Prime Minister Eden to King Hussein

I have just heard from Her Majesty's Ambassador of the action Your Majesty has taken in relieving General Glubb of his command and

[4] See Lucas (1991, p. 92).

ordering him to leave the country immediately. In view of the life-long and faithful service rendered to Jordan and your family by this officer, I feel my duty to tell Your Majesty that the resentment in Britain at this action will be widespread and deep. I cannot foretell its final consequences upon the relations between our two countries.

Avon Papers, AP20/24, Foreign Office to Amman, Cable 346, 2 March 1956

> By unfortunate coincidence, Lloyd met Nasser in Cairo on the same day. Their conversation over dinner was cordial, with Nasser offering to call off anti-British propaganda if London did not recruit any more Arab countries into the Baghdad Pact, but any benefit was lost because of a misunderstanding over Glubb's dismissal.

3.5   1956   2 March
Foreign Secretary Lloyd to Prime Minister Eden

I had a three-hour conversation with Nasser tonight in which no mention was made of developments in Amman. I did not know of the latter till I returned to the Embassy. I find it difficult to believe that Nasser did not know, but he gave no hint.

Public Record Office, FO371/121243, Cairo to Foreign Office, Cable 413, 2 March 1956

> In fact, the Egyptian President, like Lloyd, had been unaware of the events in Jordan, but further damage was done the following morning when the British Foreign Secretary returned for another discussion. Nasser, believing Britain had engineered Glubb's removal to improve its relations with Arab nationalists, offered his congratulations for the inspired manoeuvre: 'It's good, isn't it?' A confused and frustrated Lloyd could only sputter, 'What's good about it?'[5]
>
> Yet Lloyd, despite further anti-British protests in his tour of the Arabian Peninsula, still believed 'an accommodation with [Nasser] is not impossible to start on a tentative basis'.[6] Instead, it was Eden's mind that was made up. He harassed his advisers with violently-phrased messages and phone calls, insisting that Britain cease all finan-cial support of Jordan and denounce the 1948 Anglo–Jordanian

[5] Cited in Heikal (1986, p. 110).
[6] Public Record Office, FO800/734, Delhi to Commonwealth Relations Office, Cable 361, 4 March 1956.

Treaty.[7] Only the diligence of Minister of State Anthony Nutting and the Foreign Office official supervising the Middle East, Evelyn Shuckburgh, and the support of Macmillan prevented hasty British action. They persuaded the Cabinet that any abandonment of Jordan would shatter British strategy once and for all.

3.6   1956   5 March
Description by Evelyn Shuckburgh, Assistant Secretary of State in the Foreign Office, of meeting of Ministers and Foreign Office officials

Quite a big gathering round the Cabinet table. . . . We got them to accept the policy in our paper with great assistance from H. M. [Harold Macmillan] (sitting next to me) who disagreed with [Lord President] Salisbury and [Lord Privy Seal R. A.] Butler. S. [Salisbury] wants to scrap the subsidy [to Jordan] and the Treaty, but quite agrees that we must give the Iraqis a chance to see what they can do first. Rab [Butler] wants to get rid of the Treaty obligation to defend Jordan which he dislikes largely, I suspect, for pro-Israeli reasons. But H. M. wants to save what we can in Jordan. At the end he wrote on an envelope for me: 'I have gained you a day or two to rescue the work of forty years. Do try to work out a plan on which we might stay in Jordan.'

Evelyn Shuckburgh, *Descent to Suez*, London, 1986, p. 343

Far from pacified, Eden painted himself into a corner in the House of Commons on 7 March. Shuckburgh carefully drafted a speech which summarised the need to work with, rather than against, Jordan, but Eden strayed from his script to portray a Britain vigorously defending her interests against foreign threats. Unfortunately, he could not support the rhetoric with an aggressive policy and was heckled mercilessly.[8] Eden left the chamber muttering, 'Noisy, noisy',[9] as journalists pondered his imminent demise.

[7] See Lucas (1991, pp. 95–6).
[8] *Documents on International Affairs*, 1956, pp. 26–33.
[9] William Clark Papers, File 7, Clark diary, 7 March 1956.

3.7   1956   7 March
Press account of House of Commons debate

Sir Anthony suffered a blow to his prestige that was clearly reflected in the silent, devastated ranks on the Conservative benches behind him. . . . If the year goes on as it has begun, it will not be Sir Anthony but Mr Harold Macmillan who reigns in Downing Street in 1957.

Alan Thompson, *The Day Before Yesterday*, London, 1971, pp. 124–5

> The tension between Eden and the Foreign Office continued for another two weeks. When Nutting outlined a long-term policy to isolate Egypt, including a strengthened Baghdad Pact and Iraqi–Jordanian axis, installation of a pro-Western government in Syria, and a cut-off of aid to Cairo, Eden became irrational.

3.8   1956   12 March
Phone call from Prime Minister Eden to Minister of State Nutting

What's all this nonsense about isolating Nasser or 'neutralising' him, as you call it? I want him destroyed, can't you understand? I want him removed, and if you and the Foreign Office don't agree, then you'd better come to the Cabinet and explain why.

Anthony Nutting, *No End of a Lesson*, London, 1967, p. 34

> The Prime Minister was being outmanoeuvred, however. Nutting and Shuckburgh ensured that they had the support of Macmillan and thoroughly briefed Lloyd on their plans. They could also point to success: encouraged by the British, King Hussein of Jordan met Iraq's King Feisal II and his advisers on 14 March to establish a joint defence council. When Lloyd presented Nutting's policy to the Cabinet, Eden could offer no alternative and authorised the Foreign Secretary to present the package to the Americans.

3.9   1956   21 March
Cabinet decision

We should seek increased support of the Baghdad Pact and its members. We should make a further effort to persuade the US to join the Pact. We should seek to draw Iraq and Jordan more closely together. We should try to detach Saudi Arabia from Egypt by making plain to King Saud the nature of Nasser's ambitions. We should seek further support for Libya, in order to prevent the extension of Egyptian or Communist influence there. We should seek to establish in Syria a Government more friendly to the West. We should counter Egyptian subversion in the Sudan and the Persian Gulf. There were also possibilities of action aimed more directly at Egypt – e.g., the withholding of military supplies, the withdrawal of financial support for the Aswan Dam, the reduction of US economic aid, and the blocking of sterling balances.

In all this we should need the support of the US Government. The first task would be to seek Anglo-American agreement on a general realignment of policy towards Egypt.

Public Record Office, CAB128/30, C.M.24(56)

> The British approach was timely. The Eisenhower Administration was reviewing its policy in the Middle East, since Anderson had concluded that he could not arrange negotiations between Nasser and Israeli leaders. Foster Dulles told Lloyd, 'Unless Nasser [does] something soon, we [will] have to ditch him.'[10] He confirmed his intentions with a letter to Eisenhower proposing increased US support for the Baghdad Pact and financial and military support to Arab countries to align them against Cairo.[11] The President immediately agreed.

3.10   *1956   8 March*
Eisenhower diary entry

We have reached the point where it looks as if Egypt, under Nasser, is going to make no move whatsoever to meet the Israelis in an effort to settle outstanding differences. . . . It would begin to appear that our efforts should be directed towards separating the Saudi Arabians from the Egyptians and concentrating, for the moment at least, in making the former see that their best interests lie with us, and not with the Egyptians and with the Russians.

Eisenhower Library, Eisenhower Papers, Ann Whitman Series, DDE Diaries, Box 13

[10] Public Record Office, FO371/118842/JE1022/11G, Karachi to Foreign Office, Cable DORAN 33, 7 March 1956.
[11] Eisenhower Library, Eisenhower Papers, Ann Whitman Series, Dulles-Herter, Box 5, Foster Dulles to Hoover, 8 March 1956.

Eden also enlisted the President's co-operation through a series of messages. The most strident, delivered on 15 March, passed on 'absolutely reliable information' from an Egyptian working for MI6, the British foreign intelligence service. The note claimed that Egypt was trying to lead a united Arab republic by overthrowing the regimes in Iraq, Jordan, Libya, and Saudi Arabia.[12] Although the information was suspect, it reinforced Eisenhower's developing antagonism toward Egypt. So did the opinions of the President's military leaders, who warned, 'If the US does not join the Baghdad Pact, there are signs the Pact may disintegrate.'[13]

Yet the real catalyst for American policy, as Foster Dulles had told the British in January, was the death of ALPHA. After Anderson returned to Washington, Foster Dulles and his brother Allen, the Director of the CIA, consulted with their staffs on the programme against Egypt. The result was Project OMEGA, a detailed plan of diplomatic, economic, and military steps to encourage the downfall of Nasser.

3.11 *1956 28 March*
Memorandum from Secretary of State Dulles to President Eisenhower

In view of the negative outcome of our efforts to bring Colonel Nasser to adopt a policy of conciliation toward Israel, we should, I believe, now adjust certain of our Near Eastern policies, as indicated below.

The primary purpose would be to let Colonel Nasser realize that he cannot cooperate as he is doing with the Soviet Union and at the same time enjoy most-favored-nation treatment from the United States. We would want for the time being to avoid any open break which would throw Nasser irrevocably into a Soviet satellite status and we would want to leave Nasser a bridge back to good relations with the West if he so desires.

The policies indicated below would in the main be coordinated with the United Kingdom.

I. *As regards Egypt*
1 Export licenses covering arms shipments to Egypt, whether from Governmental or commercial sources, will continue to be denied by the US and the UK.

[12] Public Record Office, PREM11/1177, Eden to Eisenhower, 15 March 1956.
[13] Eisenhower Library, Eisenhower Papers, Ann Whitman Series, DDE Diaries, Box 13, March 1956 Goodpaster, Goodpaster memorandum, 15 March 1956.

2 The US and the UK will continue to delay the conclusion of current negotiations on the High Aswan Dam.

3 The US will continue to delay action on pending Egyptian requests for grains and oil. . . .

4 The US will hold in abeyance any decision on a CARE [relief] program for Egypt for 1956. . . .

5 Expanded radio facilities will be offered to Iraq to counter Egyptian broadcasts.

II. *As regards other countries*

1 The US and UK will commence negotiations with the Sudan with a view to developing – CLASSIFIED – a situation of influence in that country which would minimize Egyptian influence and its control of the head waters of the Nile.

2 Intensify present efforts to stabilize the situation in Libya.

3 Encourage the UK to maintain present treaty relationships with Jordan and help it to prevent a situation in which a pro-Egyptian coup d'etat would succeed – CLASSIFIED.

4 Give increased support to the Baghdad Pact without actually adhering to the Pact or announcing our intention of doing so. . . .

5 We will undertake an intensified program in Ethiopia to enhance the Western position in that country.

6 We will continue to take practicable steps to counter Egyptian and Soviet influence in Yemen and the other Arabian principalities. [Saudi Arabian] King Saud's assistance will be solicited.

7 The US will seem to dissuade the Israelis from . . . taking . . . precipitate steps which might bring about hostilities and thus endanger the whole Western position in the Near East to the direct advantage of the Soviets.

8 For a further indefinite period the US will continue to deny export licenses for any major military items to Israel and the adjoining Arab States. . . . We would, however, be sympathetic if other Western countries wished to sell limited quantities of defensive arms to Israel.

9 We will continue to press for effective UN action to reduce area tensions.

10 We will endeavor to strengthen pro-Western elements in Lebanon by immediately offering economic aid. . . .

11 It is extremely important that the American position in Saudi

Arabia be strengthened. . . .We will press the British to undertake a generous agreement on the Buraimi [oasis] issue, settlement of which is of paramount importance to the Western
position in Saudi Arabia.

III. In addition to the foregoing course of action, planning should be
undertaken at once with a view to possibly more drastic action in
the event that the above courses of action do not have the desired
effect. CLASSIFIED [but other documents indicate the steps
included action to prevent the sale of Egyptian cotton overseas, to
jam Egyptian radio stations, and to replace the pro-Nasser government in Syria with a pro-Western regime.]

Eisenhower Library, Eisenhower Papers, Ann Whitman Series, DDE
Diaries, Box 13

It appeared that the Anglo-American 'alliance' was not only revived
but ready to strike in the Middle East.

4

The influence of personality

Diplomatic history can reduce relations between countries to a one-dimensional plot. Tensions arise, diplomats negotiate, and Prime Ministers correspond with Presidents. Weapons are sold, economic aid offered or withdrawn, *coups* organised against unfriendly leaders. Sometimes a showdown is averted in the nick of time, sometimes war breaks out. Even the history of the Suez Crisis, with all its twists and turns, can fall prey to this pattern: Britain and the US clash bitterly, then reconcile their differences; Egypt is wooed by the West as the desirable partner then becomes the Number One enemy in the Middle East. Further chapters can be added to the story, for example, the influence of Britain's reliance upon Iraq and Jordan, but the outcome is still logical and inevitable. The only problem with the scenario is that sometimes people act neither logically nor predictably. Thus the discussion of 'personality', in combination with the records of Suez, can do more than produce interesting anecdotes for biographers. The history of the crisis takes on a complexity which cannot be predicted by any model of political behaviour.

Eden is an optimal example, his reputation as a skilful diplomat contrasting with his image as a temperamental, even irrational, Prime Minister. Even before he moved to 10 Downing Street in April 1955, Eden was known in Whitehall as a vain, highly-strung statesman. One Foreign Office official explained that the difference between Eden and his predecessor, Ernest Bevin, was that 'Bevin wouldn't throw a book at your head'. Conservative MPs spoke of a 'nervy' Eden 'always losing his temper in Cabinet, Foreign Office, and elsewhere'.[1]

This volatile nature was exacerbated by three influences. First, Eden's marriage in 1952 to Winston Churchill's niece, Clarissa, was a happy one, especially when compared with Eden's previous marriage,

[1] See Lucas (1991, p. 53).

which had ended in divorce the previous year. However, Clarissa Eden's dynamic personality added to the pressure on Eden to succeed and increased his suspicion of Cabinet colleagues.

4.1
Recollection of William Clark, Press Secretary to Prime Minister Eden, 1955–57

[Clarissa Eden] never interfered 'downstairs' at No. 10, but she resented criticism of Eden as being absolutely intolerable. She kept the door like a tiger, rarely allowing any but true and staunch friends to see him. . . . Eden had a very low boiling point and he found it a considerable strain to run one of the roughest offices in the world; the main duty of the private secretaries was to soothe him. Clarissa, on the contrary, tried to stir him up by drawing his attention to press attacks on him.

William Clark, *From Three Worlds*, London, 1986, pp. 156–7

Second, Winston Churchill's delay in transferring power to Eden, his heir apparent, was a constant irritant. When Churchill became Prime Minister in October 1951, he spoke of handing over to his Foreign Secretary within a year, but he only gave way in April 1955 when pressed by his Ministers. Eden had developed a 'constant anxiety about the Premiership [and] impatience with the Prime Minster for staying on, for fear [that] some other aspirant might overtake him in the race for the succession'.[2]

4.2
Recollection of Evelyn Shuckburgh, Private Secretary to Anthony Eden, 1951–54

A facet of Eden's worry about his succession was his intense preoccupation with what was said about him – or not said about him – in the press. . . . Neither of the Edens could wholly rid themselves of the idea that Foreign Office influence with the press, such as it was, should be used to support the Secretary of State's personal ambitions in the Government.

Evelyn Shuckburgh, *Descent to Suez*, London, 1986, p. 14

[2] Shuckburgh (1986, p. 14).

Finally, Eden was perpetually affected by his health. Throughout his career, he suffered from ailments aggravated by stress and overwork, but it was a bungled operation to remove gallstones in 1953 that nearly killed him and caused permanent damage. Two more operations partially repaired a sliced biliary duct, but bile continued to seep into Eden's blood, keeping him in constant pain and triggering periodic fevers. He soon relied on powerful painkillers, including Pethidin, normally used for women during childbirth.

4.3
Recollection of Evelyn Shuckburgh, Private Secretary to Anthony Eden, 1951–54

[Eden] was constantly having trouble with his insides. We used to carry round with us a black tin box containing various forms of analgesic supplied by his doctor, ranging from simple aspirins to morphia injections, and we dealt them out to him according to the degree of suffering. . . . When I expressed concern to his doctor about all these pain-killers, he replied that he was responsible for a very important national figure and conceived it to be his duty 'to keep him on the road'.

Evelyn Shuckburgh, *Descent to Suez*, London, 1986, p. 14

While Eden enjoyed success as Foreign Secretary, all these problems could be overcome. As one of his officials noted, 'If Eden had been run over by a bus in 1955, he would gone down in history as a great Foreign Secretary.'[3] However, Eden the Prime Minister struggled to cope with domestic issues, his relations with Cabinet colleagues were strained, and the press turned on him within six months of his accession. All the while, the Prime Minister's temper grew shorter and shorter.

4.4
Remark by R. A. Butler, Lord Privy Seal in the Eden Government, 1955–57

Anthony's father was a mad baronet and his mother a very beautiful woman. That's Anthony – half mad baronet, half beautiful woman.

Cited in Patrick Cosgrave, *R. A. Butler*, London, 1981, p. 12

---

[3] Author's interview with Sir Harold Beeley.

This temperament was especially influential upon co-operation with the Americans. Foster Dulles' predecessor as Secretary of State, Dean Acheson, was taken aback by Eden's habit of addressing everyone as 'dear', and State Department officials were also bemused by Eden's penchant for talking to flowers. The Foreign Secretary's vanity contrasted sharply with Foster Dulles' serious demeanour and quickly alienated the American advisers, one of whom said that he 'had never met a dumber man'.

4.5

Recollection of John Hanes, staff assistant to Secretary of State Dulles in 1956

Every time I saw Eden I always felt an overwhelming sense of personal vanity, and Dulles was just the opposite. Dulles may have had intellectual vanity but not personal vanity at all. Just personality-wise, they were destined not to work together; you know, [Eden's] homburg and all the rest, and his rather languid manner – a calculated English aristocracy. It wasn't Dulles' dish of tea.

Cited in Donald Neff, *Warriors at Suez*, New York, 1981, p. 145

Initially, relations between Foster Dulles and Eden were unexpectedly cordial but by 1954 they had broken down, notably over the issue of Vietnam.

The Eden of Suez was a man who, in contrast to the diplomat of the previous twenty years, reacted impetuously. He could not be certain of support from his own public and media, had tenuous backing from his colleagues, and was distrusted by his overseas allies. The personalities of Cabinet Ministers like Macmillan and Butler, not to mention the strong-willed Foster Dulles, only contributed to a situation where the quirks of individuals, rather than carefully constructed plans, shaped the outcome of the crisis.

This realm of the unpredictable was strengthened by the nature of British policymaking in 1956. Textbooks on the British Government set out a system where Prime Minister, Cabinet, Parliament, and Whitehall departments define foreign policy, but that portrayal overlooks certain features, notably the relationship between the foreign intelligence service, MI6, with the Foreign Office and the Prime Minister.

Ostensibly MI6 is part of the Foreign Office, but the arrangements for supervision were loosely structured in 1956. Liaison between MI6, the Foreign Office, and the Prime Minister was through a little-known

35

department, the Permanent Under-secretary's Department, formed in 1948. Formally, the PUSD was supervised by the Foreign Secretary and the top civil servant, the Permanent Under-secretary, but during Suez, Foreign Secretary Lloyd was occupied with diplomatic negotiations and Permanent Under-secretary Ivone Kirkpatrick took a hands-off attitude towards MI6's plans. As a result, oversight rested upon only two officials, the Deputy Under-secretary supervising the PUSD, Patrick Dean, and his deputy, Geoffrey McDermott, with McDermott increasingly cut off as the Suez crisis developed.

4.6
Remark by Archibald Ross, Assistant Secretary of State in the Foreign Office in 1956

As things began to hot up, [Eden] did take Dean over as his Foreign Office man. . . . As the crisis developed and decisions became more and more crucial, it was not so much the Foreign Office submitting advice as Eden using a member of the Foreign Office to do what he thought had to be done.

Liddell Hart Centre for Military Archives, Suez Oral History Project, interview with Archibald Ross

The result was an MI6 which might operate as a 'maverick' service, without the knowledge of the Foreign Office or the Cabinet, or as the servant of Eden's volatile temper. For example, throughout 1956, MI6 was considering the assassination of Nasser.

4.7
Intelligence officer Peter Wright's account of MI6 plans against Nasser

At the beginning of the Suez Crisis, MI6 developed a plan, through the London Station, to assassinate Nasser using nerve gas. Eden initially gave his approval to the operation, but later rescinded it when he got agreement from the French and Israelis to engage in joint military action. . . . [Two MI6 officials] told me that the London Station had an agent in Egypt with limited access to one of Nasser's headquarters. Their plan was to place canisters of nerve gas inside the ventilation system.

Peter Wright, *Spycatcher*, New York, 1987, pp. 160–1

The influence of personality

Although the Prime Minister may have rejected such contingency plans, his temperamental desire to be rid of Nasser may have encouraged MI6 to pursue the option. Eden, accompanied by high-level officers from MI6, even asked an American visitor if the Egyptian President could be shot or poisoned.

4.8
CIA official Miles Copeland's account of a meeting with MI6 Deputy Director George Young and Foreign Office official Patrick Dean in summer 1956

Eden hated Nasser. He kept bugging us. The Egyptians colonels we were dealing with wanted to have [Nasser] killed. Eden didn't think that would be such a bad idea. . . . All variety of methods had been discussed like poisoning [Nasser's] coffee.

Cited in *The Times*, 19 June 1975, p. 1

Meanwhile, MI6 pursued the overthrow of the Egyptian Government, collaborating with dissident officers in the Egyptian Army and Ministers who had been in the Government before the 1952 Revolution. Arms shipments would be buried in the desert, to be retrieved by the Egyptian conspirators when Nasser's grip on power had been weakened. There were more elaborate schemes involving other Arab countries and even Israel. Few, if any, British Ministers knew of the plotting, since there was no channel between them and the intelligence services, and it is still uncertain if Eden was informed of the plan's details.[4]

On one level, influences such as the quick temper of one man or the activities of 'secret agents' make the historian's job more difficult. Even if documents are available – in the case of MI6, only a few scraps of paper have slipped through the net of Government secrecy – they often cannot capture the nuances of personality. At the same time, simply recognising these elusive considerations advances the history of Suez, for they raise questions which previous historians could or would not answer. As the next chapter reveals, those questions and the possible answers make an interesting crisis even more intriguing.

[4] See Lucas (1991, pp. 101–3).

5

The OMEGA discussions

On 31 March 1956, two CIA representatives arrived in London for meetings with the MI6 officials overseeing Middle Eastern operations. The summary of those talks, which lasted two days, is one of the most extraordinary documents of Suez. It indicates the extent of MI6's role, which threatened Anglo-American co-operation and undermined the policy forged by the Cabinet. It also suggests that the idea of British 'collusion' with Israel against Egypt did not suddenly emerge in October 1956 but had been pursued by MI6 months earlier.

In the last days of March, both the British Government and the Eisenhower Administration agreed to a long-term policy of isolating Nasser in the Middle East before increasing economic and diplomatic pressure for his removal from power; however, George Young, the Deputy Director of MI6, immediately told the CIA envoys of his more ambitious three-phase plan.

5.1   *1956   1 April*
CIA report of meeting with MI6 officials

Following is outline our impression British Govt three-phase plan. . . .

A) *Phase One:* complete change in Government of Syria. [MI6] believes it can mount this operation alone but, if necessary, will involve joint action with Iraq, Turkey and possibly Israel. It [is] our impression that this has been discussed with the first two and possibly with third. . . .

B) *Phase Two:* Saudi Arabia. [MI6] wishes to discuss [CIA] political action potential. Believe [MI6] prepared to undertake efforts exploit splits in Royal Family and possibly utilize their position [in the] Trucial States to hasten fall of [King] Saud. Have impression they value Iraqi capabilities Saudi Arabia and believe they considering joint action with Iraqis or action behind Iraqi front in event [US Government] unwilling or unable to help out. . . .

C) *Phase Three:* to be undertaken in anticipation of violent Egyptian reaction to Phases One and Two. Have impression extent British action will be in direct proportion Egyptian reaction. This ranges from sanctions calculated to isolate Nasser to use of force (both British and Israeli) to tumble Egyptian Govt. . . . We believe extreme possibilities would involve special operations by Israelis against Egyptian supply dumps and newly acquired aircraft and tanks, as well as outright Israeli attack [on] Gaza or other border areas.

U.S. National Archives, CIA London Station to Director CIA, Cable LOND 7064

The Americans were astounded. Co-operation to replace the Syrian Government had been contemplated in OMEGA, but the US, with its air bases and oil companies in Saudi Arabia, had long relied upon King Saud's partnership. The CIA also questioned how Britain could overthrow Nasser, even with the help of countries like Turkey and Iraq. Young's repeated reference to the Israelis, 'What about the snipcocks?', was unlikely to assure Washington that this was the best way to preserve a Middle Eastern alliance against the Soviets.[1] Foster Dulles complained to colleagues, 'The British are making more drastic plans than we are.'[2]

Some of the damage caused by MI6's initiative was repaired in diplomatic and military discussions of OMEGA. The chief of the British military, Air Chief Marshal Sir William Dickson, reassured Eisenhower and Foster Dulles in a series of meetings:

5.2   1956   4 April
Memorandum of meeting between Air Chief Marshal Dickson, President Eisenhower, and Secretary of State Dulles

[Air Chief Marshal Dickson] said that when he had left London the British had been in a bit of a flap about the situation in the Middle East and felt the current was running against them. More recent messages which Sir Roger [Makins, the British Ambassador in Washington] had received since Dickson's departure from London

---

[1] See Eveland (1980, pp. 168–71).
[2] *Foreign Relations of the United States*, 1955–57, Volume XV, p. 504.

seemed to indicate that while there was serious concern, London was not in a state of flap.

Eisenhower Library, Eisenhower Papers, Ann Whitman Series, DDE Diaries, Box 15, April 1956 Goodpaster

Foreign Secretary Lloyd soon authorised a special mission to resolve the territorial dispute between Britain and Saudi Arabia over the Buraimi Oasis on the Arabian Peninsula. The US joined the Economic and Counter-Subversion Committees of the Baghdad Pact and established a liaison with the Pact's military command. The Americans and British also agreed to encourage the supply of arms to Israel through third countries. In early May, Foster Dulles and Lloyd arranged further steps in OMEGA, including the delay of funding for the High Aswan Dam and Operation STRAGGLE, a plan to change the Government in Syria.

5.3   1956   3 May
British record of meeting between Foreign Secretary Lloyd and Secretary of State Dulles in Paris

The SECRETARY OF STATE [Lloyd] asked what was the U.S. Government's intention in regard to the High Aswan Dam.

MR. DULLES said he thought the policy was to drag our feet but not to let the project drop . . . .

The SECRETARY OF STATE agreed that we should let the project languish, but without giving Nasser any excuse for saying that it was our fault . . . .

The SECRETARY OF STATE said that he felt the situation in Syria to be very serious and deteriorating. The country was already practically in Communist control.

MR. DULLES agreed that this was not far from the case.

Public Record Office, FO371/121273/V1075/117G

Yet no amount of negotiation could overcome unexpected threats to Anglo-American co-operation. Eden continued to rage about the evil of Nasser and the inaction of the Americans, complaining to Winston Churchill, '[America's] unwillingness to let it be known that we are at one on this important issue diminishes the influence which each of us could exercise in the area [the Middle East].'[3] These 'private' tantrums soon became public through the comments of newspapers like *The Times*.

[3] Public Record Office, PREM11/1690, Eden to Churchill, 21 April 1956 .

5.4   1956   14 April
Leader in The Times

The attempt to stabilise the Middle East in co-operation with Egypt is now over. Egypt has shown no desire to help. Britain must turn increasingly towards Iraq . . . and must make it clear to Egypt to non-co-operation does not pay. . . . If, while [Iraqi Prime Minister] Nuri Pasha tries to improve relations with friendly elements in Syria, Lebanon, and Jordan, [then] Britain and the United States can combine to reduce the Egyptian nuisance and check Saudi Arabian bribery, more difficult situations – and more difficult remedies – may be avoided.

'Choice of friends', *The Times*, 14 April 1956, p. 7

The Foreign Office apologised to the US Ambassador in London about the 'leaks from highest sources', but Foster Dulles still complained about 'the liability of the British situation. . . . They are so panicky.'[4] The Prime Minister only reinforced such fears by insisting on the deployment of more British troops in the Arabian Peninsula and suspending the peace-seeking mission to Saudi Arabia.[5]

Washington and London were also trying to cope with an emerging alliance between France and Israel. In October 1955, the French Ministry of Defence had agreed to supply AMX tanks and seventy-two Mystère fighter planes, among the most advanced in the world, to Israel. Shipment was delayed by objections from the French Foreign Ministry, which stressed Paris' traditional position in the Arab world, and the United States; however, the election in March 1956 of a French Government led by the Socialists, who were philosophically close to Israel's ruling Mapai Party, renewed the project. British and American pressure to limit the supply of jets brought French Foreign Minister Pineau's assurance that France would send only twenty-four Mystères to Israel, but Paris simply transferred more planes without the knowledge of Britain or the US.[6]

---

[4] US National Archives, Department of State, Central File, 684A.86/4-656, London to State Department, Cable 4467, 6 April 1956; Eisenhower Library, John Foster Dulles Papers, Telephone Calls, White House, Box 10, Eisenhower to Foster Dulles, 10 April 1956.
[5] See Lucas (1991, p. 124).
[6] See Lucas (1991, pp. 121–2, 159–60).

5.5
Recollection of General Moshe Dayan, Chief of Staff of the Israeli military in 1956

The month of April 1956 brought some relief in the form of the first few Mystère warplanes from France and the promise of more. . . . I went to France on a secret mission, together with Shimon Peres, the Director-General of the Defence Ministry, toward the end of June 1956, and after three days of talks we reached a firm agreement on the purchase of arms which would enable us to meet the quality, if not the scale, of Egypt's Soviet weaponry.

Moshe Dayan, *The Story of My Life*, London, 1976, pp. 148–9

Finally, British and American officials could not isolate themselves from public opinion. Eden's denunciation of Nasser was reinforced by a consensus among much of the press and electorate that Britain had to act decisively against the Egyptian threat. Foster Dulles had to contend with Congressmen who were angered by Egypt's recognition of Communist China and, on a more mundane level, the competition betwen Egyptian and American cotton on the world market. When the US Senate threatened to pass a bill prohibiting finance of the High Aswan Dam, Foster Dulles conceded, 'We have just about made up our minds to tell the Egyptians we will not do it.'[7] He did not anticipate that it was a decision that would trigger the Suez crisis.

---

[7] Eisenhower Library, Eisenhower Papers, Ann Whitman Series, Dulles-Herter, Box 5, Foster Dulles to Eisenhower, 16 July 1956.

6

The stakes are raised

On 19 July 1956, the Egyptian Ambassador in Washington, Ahmed Hussein, was summoned to Foster Dulles' office. The US Secretary of State, never mentioning the Congressional pressure that had forced his hand, threw an 'artificial tantrum'.

6.1   *1956   19 July*
Memorandum of meeting between Secretary of State Dulles and Ambassador Hussein

[The Secretary of State] had reluctantly come to the conclusion that it was not feasible at present for the United States to go forward with this undertaking. . . .

There were two elements which deserved special mention. First was the long-range impact of the project upon relations with the Egyptian people and Government. Implementation would impose a period of from 12 to 16 years of austerity on the part of the Egyptian people, and a major portion of Egyptian resources would have to be dedicated to this particular work. Over such a period there undoubtedly would be resentment and a feeling by the Egyptians that the limitations imposed tended to interfere with the independence which they so cherished. . . .

The other element, the Secretary said, related to the impact upon our own people. He stated in all frankness that, from the United States's standpoint, developments during the past six or seven months had not been such as to generate goodwill toward Egypt on the part of the American public. . . . We doubted that we could obtain funds from Congress to carry out the work even if the Executive Branch wished to do so. . . . No single project in the

Mutual Security Program was as unpopular today as the Aswan Dam.

US National Archives, Department of State Central Files, 874.2614/7–1956

> When Ambassador Hussein left the office, he found that the State Department had already told reporters of the withdrawal of the American offer of assistance.
>
> Contrary to the later claims of British politicians like Eden, Foster Dulles had consulted them about his action. Lloyd, who told the Cabinet on 20 July that Britain and the US 'had been forced to the conclusion that the financing of the Dam, even with the assistance which had been proposed, would be beyond Egypt's resources',[1] had warned of the possibility a few days earlier.

6.2   1956   17 July
Statement by Secretary of State Lloyd to Cabinet

It would probably be best to indicate to the Egyptians that, in view of their commitments for expenditure on armaments and military installations, the two Governments had been forced to the conclusion that the financing of the Dam, even with the assistance which had been proposed, would be beyond Egypt's resources.

Public Record Office, CAB128/30, C.M.50(56)

> The Secretary of State had also consulted briefly with Eisenhower, but the President, with little knowledge of the details, simply authorised Foster Dulles to proceed.[2]
>
> The State Department anticipated that Nasser might offer some public reaction to Foster Dulles' decision, for example, through the rejection of all technical aid from the US, but the Egyptian President, 'surprised by the insulting attitude with which the refusal was declared', soon considered the more dramatic step of nationalising the Suez Canal Company.[3] The Egyptians were due to take over the Canal's operations in 1968 when the Company's concession to supervise shipping expired, but for Nasser immediate nationalisation was a symbolic response proving that Egypt was not at the mercy of American or British decisions. Through a careful study of the military situation, he realised that Britain, even with French co-operation, would need weeks

[1] Public Record Office, CAB128/30, C.M.51(56), 20 July 1956.
[2] See Neff (1981, p. 260).
[3] See Lucas (1991, pp. 137–40).

to assemble the equipment and troops necessary to occupy the Canal Zone, and he believed that, as time passed, the British public would tire of the prospect of war and push the Government into negotiations with Egypt. Under no circumstances, Nasser concluded, would Eden accept Israeli participation in military operations.

6.3

Account by Mohammed Heikal, adviser to President Nasser, of Nasser's decision-making in July 1956

Nasser started from the premise that Eden was weak – weak in character, weak in his position in his party and government, and weak in his standing in the country. Nasser calculated that, like many essentially weak men, Eden was attracted by the idea of doing something violent. . . . But if he was to take advantage of these favourable circumstances Eden would have to act very quickly. The period of maximum danger for Egypt, Nasser believed, would be in the first few days after nationalization of the Suez Canal Company had been proclaimed. He thought that up to, say, 10 August there would be a 90 per cent risk of an armed attack on Egypt; for the rest of August the risk would decline to about 80 per cent; in September it would be down to 60 per cent; in the first half of October to 40 per cent; in the second half to 20 per cent, and thereafter, thanks to the mobilization of world opinion which Nasser confidently looked forward to, the risk would virtually evaporate.

Mohammed Heikal, *Cutting the Lion's Tail*, London, 1986, p. 133

Bolstered by this assessment, Nasser assured a crowd in Cairo on 24 July, 'I will tell you on Thursday, God willing, how Egypt has acted so that all its projects . . . may be projects of sovereignty, dignity, and not those of humiliation, slavery, domination, rule, and exploitation.'[4] Two days later, on the fourth anniversary of the Egyptian Revolution, he addressed 250,000 people in Menshiyeh Square in Alexandria. In a speech of two and a half hours, he reviewed the history of the Suez Canal and the story of the High Aswan Dam and then, true to his promise, concluded with the announcement that Egyptian personnel had seized the offices of the Suez Canal Company.

---

[4] Cited in Hoopes (1973, p. 345).

6.4   1956   26 July
Speech by President Nasser

After the past four years, and as we celebrate the fifth year of the revolution, we feel . . . that we are stronger and more resolute in our determination, power, and faith. . . . We now feel that we are realising our glory and our grandeur. The people of Egypt alone shall be sovereign in Egypt. We shall march forward united and in solidarity like one nation having faith in itself and in its homeland, and faith also in its strength. . . .

At this moment as I talk to you, some of your Egyptian brethren are proceeding to administer the canal company and to run its affairs. They are taking over the canal company at this very moment – the Egyptian canal company, not the foreign canal company. . . . They are now carrying out this task so that we can make up for the past and build new edifices of grandeur and dignity. May the Almighty grant you success, and may the peace and blessing of God be upon you.

Documents on International Affairs, 1956, pp. 77–113

> The crowd responded with a ten-minute ovation and chants of 'Long live Nasser, Lord and Saviour of the Arabs.' An observer from the British Embassy noted that all that remained in the Square after the celebrations was a float of 'the Sphinx swallowing a British soldier with the British flag sewn on his derrière'.[5]
>
> Ironically, Eden was dining with Nasser's rivals, King Feisal II of Iraq and Prime Minister Nuri Sa'id, when news came of the nationalisation. After bidding his guests goodnight, the Prime Minister summoned other Ministers and his military Chiefs of Staff, as well as the Acting US Ambassador, to 10 Downing Street. The initial mood was defiant.

6.5   1956   27 July
Cable by Andrew Foster, official in US Embassy in London, to State Department

Cabinet takes an extremely grave view of situation and very strong feelings were expressed, especially by Eden, to the effect that Nasser must not be allowed to get away with it. . . . As meeting broke up Lloyd told me he himself was moving towards conclusion that only

[5] See Lucas (1991, p. 139).

solution lay in a Western consortium taking over and operating the Canal, establishing itself if need be by military force.

Eisenhower Library, Eisenhower Papers, Ann Whitman Series, Dulles-Herter, Box 5, London to State Department, Cable 481

> Frustration set in, however, over the military's ability to fulfil such wishes. The last British troops in the Suez Canal Zone had left in June 1956, many soldiers were out of training or fighting guerrillas in Cyprus, and equipment was out-of-date or malfunctioning.

6.6   1956   27 July
Recollection of William Clark, Press Secretary to Prime Minister Eden, of meeting

The question that Eden put perfectly clearly was when we can take military action to topple Nasser, free the Canal. . . . The answers that he got, which were slightly horrifying, were that we could not do this. . . . Britain had the capacity to deal with Mau Mau [insurgents in Kenya] or with the Doomsday with an atomic war, [but] we did not have plans for a little local episode in the Eastern Mediterranean.

BBC radio broadcast, *Neither War nor Peace at 10 Downing Street*, 1979

> With Britain unable to act alone, as the Acting US Ambassador recorded, 'the question confronting Cabinet tonight was, of course, [the] extent to which US would go in supporting and participating in firm position *vis-à-vis* Nasser in terms of economic sanctions and, beyond that if necessary, military action'.[6] The next day, Eden asked Eisenhower for assistance.

6.7   1956   27 July
Letter from Prime Minister Eden to President Eisenhower

This morning I have reviewed the whole position with my Cabinet colleagues and Chiefs of Staff. We are all agreed that we cannot afford to allow Nasser to seize control of the Canal in this way, in defiance of international agreements. If we take a firm stand over

---

[6] Eisenhower Library, Eisenhower Papers, Ann Whitman Series, Dulles-Herter, Box 5, London to State Department, Cable 481, 27 July 1956.

this now, we shall have the support of all the maritime powers. If we do not, our influence and yours throughout the Middle East will, we are concerned, be further destroyed. . . . My colleagues and I are convinced that we must be ready, in the last resort, to use force to bring Nasser to his senses.

Eisenhower Library, Eisenhower Papers, Ann Whitman Series, International, Box 19

> The Americans were ill-prepared for Nasser's nationalisation and Eden's appeal. Eisenhower, who had had little to do with American policy in the Middle East, was in charge: Foster Dulles was visiting Peru and the President decided that the situation did not require the Secretary of State's immediate return to Washington. Eisenhower had some sympathy for British feelings since 'no nation is likely to allow its nationals to be held in what amounts to slavery, operations of the Canal may suffer, and we and many other countries have a concern over its operations', but he could not decide upon any action. Instead, Foster Dulles' deputy, Herbert Hoover, Jr., stepped into the vacuum. Like his father, who was the US President from 1929 to 1933, Hoover had never had much sympathy for Britain's global position.

6.8   1956   28 July
Cable from Under-secretary of State Hoover to Secretary of State Dulles

At conference with President this afternoon I pointed out grave dangers of engaging in military intervention on grounds outlined by Eden and that while strong position should be taken to preserve Western status in Middle East, I did not believe confiscation of company was in itself sufficient reason for military invasion. Some other overt act would be necessary before we would be justified in adopting such measures. Otherwise our entire posture would be compromised. President agreed.

US National Archives, Department of State, Central Files, 974.7301/7–2856, State Department to Lima, Cable TEDUL 20

7

The dance of diplomacy

Initial reactions in London and Washington set a pattern which would recur throughout the Suez Crisis. While the Eden Government constructed the rationale for force and asked the Americans for support, the Eisenhower Administration, stopping short of a blunt refusal, tried to delay any final decision. The British Cabinet recognised that, 'from a narrow legal point of view, [Nasser's] action amounted to no more than a decision to buy out the shareholders', but it quickly adopted a new basis for intervention.

7.1 *1956 27 July*
Cabinet meeting

The Canal was a vital link between the East and the West, and its importance as an international waterway, recognised in the [Constantinople] Convention signed in 1888, had increased with the development of the oil industry and the dependence of the world on oil supplies. It was not a piece of Egyptian property but an international asset of the highest importance, and it should be managed as an international trust.

Public Record Office, CAB128/30, C.M.54(56)

Using this rationale, the Egypt Committee, Britain's 'War Cabinet' during the crisis, authorised the Chancellor of the Exchequer, Harold Macmillan, to seize Egyptian assets in Britain, prepared military forces to move to the Middle East, and endorsed discussions with France about further action.[1] In contrast, Eisenhower and Hoover sent the Deputy Under-secretary of State, Robert Murphy, to London for meetings with Lloyd and French Foreign Secretary Christian Pineau.

[1] Public Record Office, CAB134/1216, E.C.(56)4th meeting, 30 July 1956.

The contrast in the strategies was soon evident. Pineau bluntly told Murphy that France would go to war because of Nasser's support for rebels in Algeria who were challenging French authority: 'One successful battle in Egypt would be worth ten in North Africa.' Lloyd was more careful in his expression but just as adamant.

7.2   1956   29 July
Record of meeting between Foreign Secretary Lloyd, Foreign Minister Pineau, and Deputy Under-secretary of State Murphy

[Lloyd said that] while Western position in Middle East will be jeopardized if Nasser gets away with his action. NATO, Western Europe and other parts of world will be at mercy of man who has shown himself irresponsible and faithless. We should be careful to place matter in correct perspective. . . . [The British Government] has taken decision to arrange to have it within its power to use force. We may come rather quickly to point where decision must be made to act.

US National Archives, Department of State, Central Files, 974.7301/7–2956, London to State Department, Cable 521

Murphy was further distressed in discussion with other British Ministers such as Eden and Macmillan.

7.3   1956   31 July
Cable from Deputy Under-secretary of State Murphy to State Department on meetings with British Ministers

[Eden and Macmillan] said British government has decided to drive Nasser out of Egypt. The decision, they declared, is firm. . . . Macmillan repeated over and over in language similar to that employed by Eden that Government had taken the decision and that Parliament and British people are with them.
[. . .]
Macmillan indulged in [a very] graphic dissertation on British past history and stressed that if [Britain] had to go down now, the Government and . . . British people would rather do so on this issue than become perhaps another Netherlands.

US National Archives, Department of State, Central Files, 674.84A/ 7–3156, London to State Department, Cable 550, 31 July 1956

Informed of this reaction by Murphy, Eisenhower countered that 'the British [are] out of date in thinking of this as a mode of action in the present circumstances',[2] and Foster Dulles, having returned from Peru, was sent to London to arrange an international conference. He carried with him a letter from Eisenhower that stressed the US would not support military action without an attempt at a negotiated solution.

7.4   1956   31 July
Letter from President Eisenhower to Prime Minister Eden

We recognize the transcendent worth of the Canal to the free world and the possibility that eventually the use of force might become necessary in order to protect international rights. But we have been hopeful that through a Conference in which would be represented the signatories to the [Suez Canal] Convention of 1888, as well as other maritime nations, there would be brought about such pressures on the Egyptian government that the efficient operation of the Canal could be assured for the future.

For my part, I cannot over-emphasize the strength of my conviction that some such method must be attempted before action such as you contemplate should be undertaken. If unfortunately the situation can finally be resolved only by drastic means, there should be no grounds for belief anywhere that corrective measures were undertaken merely to protect national or individual investors, or the legal rights of a sovereign nation were ruthlessly flouted. A conference, at the very least, should have a great educational effect throughout the world. Public opinion here and, I am convinced, in most of the world, would be outraged should there be a failure to make such efforts. Moreover, initial military successes might be easy, but the eventual price might become far too heavy.

Eisenhower Library, Eisenhower Papers, Ann Whitman Series, International, Box 19

Foster Dulles has often been accused of insensitivity to British feelings, but he was careful to phrase the American rejection of immediate force in terms that would be acceptable to the Eden Government. He told Lloyd, for example, that 'a way had to be found to make Nasser disgorge what he was attempting to swallow'. The US 'did not exclude the

[2] Eisenhower Library, Eisenhower Papers, Ann Whitman Series, DDE Diaries, Box 16, July 1956 Diary, Staff Memoranda, Goodpaster memorandum, 31 July 1956.

use of force' but only 'if all other methods failed'.[3] The Secretary of State repeated this assurance of support for the British case, if not for military action, to Eden in two meetings on 1–2 August.

7.5   1956   1 August
Secretary of State Dulles' record of meeting with Prime Minister Eden

[Eden] went on to express his Government's view that prompt forcible action was necessary. He said that if Nasser 'got away with it', it would mean disaster for British interests in the whole Middle East, and France felt the same way with respect to their interests in North Africa. . . .

I said that I agreed that Nasser should not 'get away with it', but the question was how his course should be reversed and he could be brought to 'disgorge'. I said that United States public opinion was not ready to back a military venture by Britain and France which, at this stage, could be plausibly portrayed as motivated by imperialist and colonialist ambitions in the general area. . . .

US National Archives, Department of State, Central Files, 974.7301/8–156, Foster Dulles memorandum, 1 August 1956

The approach was understood by Lloyd, but it produced a near-catastrophic misunderstanding with Eden, who forgot Foster Dulles' proviso that force might be used 'if all other methods failed'. Instead, he implied to the press that military action was a primary option since 'Dulles freely committed himself to the stand that the Canal should not be left in the sole control of Egypt'.[4]

The immediate situation was resolved through Foster Dulles' deliberations with Lloyd and Pineau. They eventually agreed that twenty-four countries, including Egypt and the Soviet Union, would be invited to London on 16 August in 'a genuine effort to enable relevant free world opinion to express itself on the subject of international operation of the Suez Canal'.[5] However, the Eden Government remained under pressure, partly of its own making, to strike Cairo. Macmillan,

[3] PRO, PREM11/1098, Lloyd–Foster Dulles meeting, 1 August 1956; US National Archives, Department of State, Central File, 974.7301/7-3156, Murphy memorandum, 1 August 1956.
[4] Cited in MacDonald (1976, p. 265).
[5] Public Record Office, FO371/119092/JE14211/423G and 424G, Lloyd–Pineau–Foster Dulles meetings, 2 August 1956.

referring to the appeasement of the 1930s, intoned, 'No one wanted to see another Munich.'[6] Most of the British press agreed.

7.6   1956   1 August
Leader in *The Times*

If Nasser is allowed to get away with his coup, all the British and other Western interests in the Middle East will crumble. Quibbling over whether or not [Nasser] was 'legally entitled' to make the grab will delight the finicky and comfort the faint-hearted but entirely misses the issues.

'The hinge of history', *The Times*, 1 August 1956, p. 9

> Even more significant was the apparent support for the Government from the Labour Party. In a famous speech in the House of Commons on 2 August, the Labour leader Hugh Gaitskell compared the threat from Nasser to that from the dicatators of the 1930s. The rhetoric overshadowed Gaitskell's subsequent statement, which would become important later in the crisis, that any British action against Egypt must have the support of the United Nations.

7.7   1956   2 August
Statement by Leader of the Opposition Gaitskell to the House of Commons

This episode must be recognised as part of the struggle for the mastery of the Middle East. . . . It is all very familiar. It is exactly the same that we encountered from Mussolini and Hitler in those years before the war.

Hansard, House of Commons, 2 August 1956, Vol. 557, Col. 1613

> The true intention of British planning was confirmed in the days before the London Conference. Writing to Eisenhower again, Eden adopted Gaitskell's comparison of Nasser to Mussolini and insisted, 'The removal of Nasser and installation of a regime less hostile to the West must therefore also rank high among our objectives.'[7] Meanwhile,

---

[6] US National Archives, Department of State, Central File, 974.7301/8-156, Murphy and Aldrich memoranda, 1 August 1956.
[7] Public Record Office, PREM11/1098, Foreign Office to Washington, Cable 3568, 5 August 1956.

Macmillan was the first Minister to urge military co-operation with Israel.

7.8   1956   3 August
Letter from Chancellor of the Exchequer Macmillan to Prime Minister Eden

If I were in [Israel's] position I should certainly intervene and get all the advantage I could. All history shows that statesmen of any character will seize a chance like this and the Jews have character. They are bound to do something.

Surely what matters is that what they should do is to help us and not hinder us. We don't want them to go off and attack Jordan.

Cited in Alistair Horne, *Macmillan: Volume I, 1894–1956*, London, 1988, p. 401

The Egypt Committee rejected the idea, an angry Eden commenting that it was 'none of [Macmillan's] business anyway',[8] but the Chancellor had other plans. The British military, assuming that they were merely to seize the Suez Canal Zone, had recommended an assault upon Port Said at the northern end of the Canal, but Macmillan argued for a direct assault upon the cities of Cairo and Alexandria since the real objective was to overthrow Nasser. Once more Eden was infuriated with the Chancellor's persistence; however, Macmillan had prepared his case carefully, consulting Winston Churchill and British military commanders. The Egypt Committee approved the change in operations, codenamed MUSKETEER.[9]

On 8 August, Eden broadcast to the nation on radio and television. His temper was not helped by the cramped, hot studio and the glare which 'convinced [him] that those Communists on the BBC were shining the lights into his eyes'.[10] The speech turned into a strident challenge to Nasser.

7.9   1956   8 August
Broadcast by Prime Minister Eden

We cannot agree than an act of plunder which threatens the livelihood of many nations shall be allowed to succeed, and we must

---

[8] See Lucas (1991, pp. 158–9).
[9] See Lucas (1991, pp. 160–2).
[10] BBC, *Television and Number 10* (1988), interview with William Clark.

make sure that the life of the great trading nations of the world cannot, in the future, be strangled at any moment by some interruption to the free passage of the Canal. . . . Our quarrel is not with Egypt, still less with the Arab world; it is with Colonel Nasser.

Documents on International Affairs, 1956, pp. 158–61

The broadcast worried the Americans and prompted Gaitskell to remind Eden that nationalisation of the Canal was 'only a threat not, in my opinion, justifying retaliation by war'.[11] At the same time, the speech bolstered the alliance with the French and accelerated military preparations. The question no longer seemed to be if the attack would be launched but when. Eden was throwing 'terrible tantrums', berating his officials in late-night phone calls and threatening direct control of the 'subversive' BBC because it reported Nasser's statements.[12]

7.10
Recollection of Richard Powell, Permanent Under-secretary at the Ministry of Defence

[Eden] was very jumpy, very nervous, very wrought up. . . . He regarded almost the destiny of the world as resting on his shoulders. . . . I had to have a scrambler telephone installed in my flat so that he could ring me up and talk about these things.

Liddell Hart Centre for Military Archives, Suez Oral History Project, interview with Richard Powell

Foster Dulles' second mission in three weeks to restrain the British was straightforward. If the Eden Government could be assured that the Canal would come under international control, with Egypt receiving no profits from her nationalisation, then an invasion was unnecessary. On the surface, the London Conference met these objectives. Representatives of twenty-two nations attended – Egypt and Greece declined their invitations – and eighteen of them accepted the proposal for international operation of the Canal.

[11] Public Record Office, PREM11/1159, Gaitskell to Eden, 10 August 1956.
[12] See Lucas (1991, pp. 166–8).

7.11   1956   23 August
Resolution adopted by London Maritime Conference

The Governments approving this Statement . . . affirm that, as stated in the Preamble of the Convention of 1888, there should be established a 'definite system destined to guarantee at all times, and for all the Powers, the free use of the Canal'.

Such a system, which would be established with due regard to the sovereign rights of Egypt, should assure efficient and dependable operation, maintenance and development of the Canal as a free, open, and secure international waterway in accordance with the principles of the Convention of 1888. . . .

Documents on International Affairs, 1956, pp. 175–7

> The proposal was to be presented to Nasser by a five-member committee led by Australian Prime Minister Robert Menzies.
>
> This solution was deceptively simple, however. On the one hand, Foster Dulles had to assure British Ministers that 'international control' would be achieved even if Nasser refused the eighteen-nation resolution. Thus Eden, after lunch with Foster Dulles, wrote that the Secretary of State 'seemed not to exclude the possibility of joint use of force'[13] and Macmillan claimed Foster Dulles 'really agreed with our position'.[14] On the other hand, Foster Dulles was under great pressure to seek 'international supervision', with Egypt still in charge of operations, rather than 'international control'. Eisenhower favoured the approach as did several of the eighteen countries who accepted the London plan.[15] Since Foster Dulles could only steer a middle course if he avoided the details of 'international control', his strategy merely left others groping for the term's meaning.
>
> Even before the London Conference ended, Eden's optimism faltered.

7.12   1956   18 August
Remarks by Prime Minister Eden at Egypt Committee meeting

[There was] little more that the US Government could do in the way of exerting economic pressure. . . . [Foster Dulles] was not in favour of provoking Colonel Nasser into taking further action which

---

[13] Public Record Office, CAB134/1216, E.C.(56)16th meeting, 16 August 1956.

[14] Cited in Horne (1988, p. 408).

[15] Eisenhower Library, John Foster Dulles Papers, White House Memoranda, Chronological, Box 5, Foster Dulles memorandum, 14 August 1956.

would justify the use of military force. . . . The US Government could not justify going to war over oil in the Middle East.

Public Record Office, CAB134/1216, E.C.(56)18th meeting

> After the Conference, Lloyd suggested to Foster Dulles that 'Colonel Nasser . . . would look a fool if he could not lay his hands on any dues' from shipping through the Canal, but the US Secretary of State objected that Nasser would refuse passage, forcing ships to go around the southern tip of Africa and driving up the price of oil and other commodities. He concluded, 'It would be impossible to take any of these measures without preparing public opinion in the US'[16]
>
> So would Britain proceed with its military plan? The question divided Ministers and officials. Some began to consider acting without the US Lord Salisbury, a senior Cabinet member, told Macmillan, 'It must, I feel, now be for the Foreign Office to produce one [provocation] which is likely to exasperate Nasser to such an extent that he does something to give us an excuse for marching in.'[17] Yet, for others, the speed with which the Cabinet approved military preparations in the days after nationalisation was causing concern, especially as the 'inner circle' of the Egypt Committee had taken over all deliberations. Several Ministers wrote to Eden with their concerns, while R. A. Butler, the Lord Privy Seal and former Chancellor, became 'a very damp influence' upon the Government.

7.13   *1956   24 August*
Letter from Lord Salisbury, the Lord President, to Prime Minister Eden

Both you and I knew that [Monckton] had, for some time, had doubts about a firm policy over Suez, but I suspect that there will be a measure of support for his views. . . . Rab [Butler] is clearly not happy, and I gather . . . that he has been making enquiries and finds there are quite a number of others, especially among the younger members of the Cabinet, who have not yet made up their minds.

Public Record Office, PREM11/1152

> The issue came to a head in the Egypt Committee on 24 August. Eden and Macmillan asked for a commitment that Nasser's rejection of the

[16] Public Record Office, PREM11/1099, Lloyd–Foster Dulles–Pineau meeting, 23 August 1956.
[17] Cited in Horne (1988, p. 427).

eighteen-power plan, followed by the United Nations' formal support for international control of the Canal, would be sufficient for the use of force. To accelerate the process, they requested the authority to order military operations before the decision of the United Nations was announced. The Minister of Defence, Walter Monckton, objected that the 'Prime Minister and Chancellor were trying to rush things through. . . . He could not agree to press the button now, which made war inevitable.' Eden, supported by most of the Egypt Committee, responded that Britain 'had no alternative' but to 'secure the defeat of Nasser by one method or another'.

7.14   1956   24 August
Egypt Committee meeting

In discussion it was stated that . . . it would be desirable to examine the possibility of reducing the present 17-day interval in the military time-table by moving certain forces to the Mediterrranean at an earlier date as part of the preliminary moves for mounting any operations, should they be required.

Public Record Office, CAB134/1216, E.C.(56) 21st meeting

Monckton was isolated within the Committee, but if he allied with Butler and discontented junior Ministers, there could be a Cabinet rebellion. So Eden, pushed by his supporters, took the question to the Cabinet on 28 August. The outcome was a decisive victory for the Prime Minister. Skilfully, he told the Cabinet that Britain would take its case to the United Nations Security Council 'if the support of the US and others was assured', and Macmillan presented invasion as a defensive manoeuvre, since the costs of the operations were small compared to a cut-off of British oil through the Suez Canal and Middle Eastern pipelines. Thus, when Monckton complained about the ill effects of force, Lord Salisbury could respond by linking the British appeal to the Security Council and any subsequent assault: 'Before any military measures were taken, we should have recourse to the procedures of the United Nations, but if the United Nations failed to secure international justice, it would have failed to fulfil its purpose.' Instead of leading the opposition, Butler cautiously said that the Egypt Committee 'should be able to show that, before resorting to force, they had taken all practicable steps to secure a satisfactory settlement by peaceful means'.

7.15   1956   28 August
Cabinet meeting

The Prime Minister, summing up this part of the discussion, said that it was evident that the Cabinet were united in the view that the frustration of Colonel Nasser's policy was a vital British interest which must be secured, in the last resort, by the use of force. He fully recognised that, before recourse was had to force, every practicable attempt should be made to secure a satisfactory settlement by peaceful means and it must be made clear to the public, here and overseas, that no effort to this end had been spared. At the same time we could not afford to allow these efforts to impose an undue delay.

Public Record Office, CAB128/30, C.M.62(56)

Other groups within the Government were also proceeding with their plans for Nasser's demise. MI6 had suffered a blow when the Egyptians broke up their operations in Cairo, arresting thirty people and expelling two officials of the British Embassy, but the agency persisted in its contacts with Egyptian military officers opposed to Nasser. For example, on 27 August, Julian Amery, a Conservative MP and Macmillan's son-in-law, and two MI6 officers met conspirators in France. The soldiers then conferred with leading Egyptian civilians about the assassination of Nasser and his closest advisers and the installation of a Government led by Saleh ed-Din, the Egyptian Foreign Minister from 1950 to 1952.

7.16
Recollections of Julian Amery MP of British contacts with Egyptian opponents of President Nasser

[The Egyptian opposition's] plan was not to overthrow [Nasser] because they did not think that this was on but they thought that [Nasser] would have gone and then they would have taken over and come out and said, 'Don't come to Cairo, we'll have an international conference: you are in charge of the Canal at the moment, but we will make a new plan.'

Liddell Hart Centre for Military Archives, Suez Oral History Project, interview with Julian Amery

One way or another, the British were determined to have the last laugh over Nasser.

8

On the brink?

On 3 September, the Menzies Committee presented the eighteen-power plan of the London Conference to Nasser. While the initial talks were amiable, with Menzies imitating Winston Churchill to entertain the Egyptian President, there was no chance of agreement. Menzies, gruff and forceful, presented the ultimatum of accepting the plan or facing invasion. Nasser replied that 'if Menzies was trying to convey the idea that rejection of these proposals would lead to trouble, he was quite prepared to let it come at once'.[1] Menzies wanted to break off the talks then and there; only the efforts of the other Committee members prolonged the discussions for several days.[2]

8.1 *1956   9 September*
Cable from Prime Minister Menzies to Prime Minister Eden

Egypt is not only a dictatorship, but it has all the earmarks of a Police state. The tapping of telephone lines, the installation of microphones, the creation of a vast body of security police – all these things are accepted as commonplace. . . .

So far from being charming, [Nasser] is rather gauche, with some irritating mannerisms, such as rolling his eyes up to the ceiling when he is talking to you and producing a quick, quite evanescent grin when he can think of nothing else to do.

Public Record Office, PREM11/1101

Under the schedule it had just agreed, the Eden Government planned perfunctory talks at the United Nations to establish the pretext for

[1] Cited in Heikal (1986, p. 166).
[2] US National Archives, Department of State, Central File, 974.7301/9-556, Cairo to State Department, Cable 613, 5 September 1956.

force. Yet once more it faced the question of American support, for the US only had to veto any British resolution in the Security Council to prevent military action. To win over Eisenhower, Eden invoked the Communist threat, but the President, in a letter drafted by Foster Dulles, simply replied that any invasion would alienate world opinion, strengthening Nasser and his supporters in Moscow.[3] Desperate, Eden continued the exchange on 6 September by portraying Egypt as the puppet of a Soviet Union which was as dangerous as Nazi Germany in the 1930s.

8.2   1956   6 September
Letter from Prime Minister Eden to President Eisenhower

In the 1930's [*sic*] Hitler established his position by a series of carefully planned movements. These began with the occupation of the Rhineland and were followed by successive acts of aggression against Austria, Czechoslovakia, Poland and the West. His actions were tolerated and excused by the majority of the population of Western Europe. . . .

In more recent years Russia has attempted similar tactics. The blockade of Berlin was to have been the opening move in a campaign designed at least to deprive the Western powers of their whole position in Germany. On this occasion we fortunately reacted at once with the result that the Russian design was never unfolded. But I am sure that you would agree that it would be wrong to infer from this circumstance that no Russian design existed. Similarly the seizure of the Suez Canal is, we are convinced, the opening gambit in a planned campaign designed by Nasser to expel all Western influence and interests from Arab countries. He believes that, if he can get away with this and if he can successfully defy eighteen nations, his prestige in Arabia will be so great that he will be able to mount revolutions of young officers in Saudi Arabia, Jordan, Syria and Iraq. (We know from our joint sources that he is already preparing a revolution in Iraq which is the most stable and progressive.) These new Governments will in effect be Egyptian satellites if not Russian ones. They will have to place their united oil resources under the control of a united Arabia led by Egypt and under Russian influence. When that moment

---

[3] Public Record Office, PREM11/1177, Eden to Eisenhower, 27 August 1956, and Eisenhower to Eden, 3 September 1956.

comes Nasser can deny oil to Western Europe and we here shall all be at his mercy.

Public Record Office, PREM11/1177

The Americans had no intention of giving way, but Foster Dulles warned Eisenhower that his talks with Eden, Macmillan, and Lloyd indicated that 'the British were determined to move militarily unless there was clear acceptance of the 18-Power plan by Nasser by around the 10th of September'.[4] On a weekend vacation in Canada, the Secretary of State devised another proposal for negotiation. Countries using the Canal could supply pilots for ships. Any problems with passage would be handled by warships stationed at either end of the waterway. If Egypt did not keep the Canal clear of obstructions, the user nations had a right to control it under an 1888 agreement, the Constantinople Convention.

8.3 1956 4 September
Secretary of State Dulles to John Coulson, the British Minister in Washington

The users would run the Canal themselves. . . . Nasser would thus see the dollars slip out of his hands. He was much more likely to be deflated by the loss of these revenues than by the threat of force.

Public Record Office, PREM11/1100, Washington to Foreign Office, Cable 1804, 4 September 1956

The Egypt Committee had to act quickly. MUSKETEER, the plan to invade Alexandria and Cairo, could not be launched after 6 October because of deteriorating weather in the Mediterranean. With seventeen days needed between a decision to attack and the actual landing, the order had to be given by 19 September. In short, the British did not have enough time, after Nasser's rejection of the Menzies mission, to complete discussions in the United Nations and convene a special session of Parliament to authorise the invasion. Military leaders and politicians were also beginning to worry that the high level of Egyptian casualties in the assault on the cities would turn world opinion against Britain.

---

[4] Eisenhower Library, John Foster Dulles Papers, White House Memoranda, Chronological, Box 5, Meetings with the President, August–December 1956 (7), Foster Dulles memorandum, 29 August 1956.

General Charles Keightley, the Commander-in-Chief of MUSKE-TEER, met these problems with a new plan, MUSKETEER REVISE, which could be maintained until the end of October and required only eight days between decision and implementation. Instead of the deadly landing at Alexandria and advance upon Cairo, the British would use aerial and naval bombardment, supported by propaganda, to break down Egyptian resistance to Western operation of the Suez Canal and enable Allied forces to secure the Canal Zone. Only then would British and French troops enter Cairo to establish a military government. Eden, who wanted a quick strike against Egyptian cities, was incensed with Keightley, but unable to establish the diplomatic pretext for the original MUSKETEER, he had to give way.[5]

With the extra month of manoeuvre allowed by REVISE, the Egypt Committee could consider the Users Association. Foster Dulles had assured British representatives that, with the Association, 'we could get Nasser down' and promised not only stronger economic sanctions against Egypt but also emergency oil shipments to Britain if Nasser blocked the Canal.[6] Lloyd replied, via the US Embassy in London, 'The UK Government is particularly pleased with the Secretary's plan for an association of canal users because it consti-tutes a "slap in the face" for Nasser.'[7] On 10 September, the Egypt Committee authorised the change in both military planning and diplomatic strategy.

8.4   1956   10 September
Egypt Committee meeting

The Committee agreed that detailed plans should now be prepared on the concept of operations as set out in the memorandum by the Minister of Defence [for Operation REVISE] and that plans for Operation Musketeer should be shelved. . . .

Mr. Dulles' proposal for a 'users' club' were ingenious and, although it would take some time to determine whether they offered a way to a solution of the dispute, it would be worthwhile exploring them. . . .

Public Record Office, CAB134/1216, E.C.(56)26th meeting

[5] See Lucas (1991, pp. 188–90).
[6] Public Record Office, PREM11/1100, Washington to Foreign Office, Cables 1838 and 1845–47, 8–9 September 1956.
[7] US National Archives, Department of State, Central File, 684A.86/9-1156, London to State Department, Cable 1410, 11 September 1956.

Yet even before Eden revealed the initiative to the House of Commons, Foster Dulles had dashed British hopes. Presented with Eden's draft announcement that 'users could take such steps as seemed fitting to them to enforce their rights', the Secretary of State told the British Ambassador, Roger Makins, that the US could not commit itself to that provision. Furthermore, the Eisenhower Administration could not force US-owned ships under the flags of other countries to withhold transit dues from Egypt. Since ninety to ninety-five percent of American cargoes flew under other flags, Foster Dulles had effectively undercut any economic sanctions against Nasser.[8] Eisenhower, at a press conference, rubbed salt in the British wound by refusing to endorse Anglo-French military action if traffic through the Canal broke down.[9]

The situation went from bad to worse when Eden, in the House of Commons, highlighted the threat of force. He concluded, '[We must] check aggression by the pressure of international opinion, if possible, but, if not, by other means before it has grown to monstrous proportions.'[10] Foster Dulles angrily retaliated by declaring to reporters that, even if Egypt hindered the Users Association, 'we do not intend to shoot our way through'.[11] Publicly deprived of American support, Eden indicated to the Commons the next day that Britain would refer any question of force to the United Nations.

8.5   1956   13 September
Statement by Prime Minister Eden in the House of Commons

Would HMG give a pledge not to use force except after reference to the Security Council? . . . It would certainly be our intention, if circumstances allowed, or in other words, except in an emergency, to refer a matter of that kind to the Security Council. Beyond that, I do not think that any Government can possibly go.

Hansard, House of Commons, 13 September 1956, Vol. 558, Col. 307

The Prime Minister's previous promise of strong action now seemed hollow, and the press labelled his statement a 'climbdown'.[12]

---

[8] Public Record Office, PREM11/1101, Washington to Foreign Office, Cables 1869, 1873, 1875, and 1879, 11 September 1956.
[9] Public Record Office, PREM11/1101, Washington to Foreign Office, Cable 1891, 11 September 1956.
[10] Hansard, 12 September 1956, Vol. 558, Cols. 1–15.
[11] Public Record Office, PREM11/1101, Washington to Foreign Office, Cable 1916, 13 September 1956.
[12] See Clark (1986, p. 188).

Anglo-French plans now depended upon a walkout by the 165 non-Egyptian pilots of the Egyptian Canal Authority, but against all expectations, the Authority maintained the flow of traffic with the remaining forty Egyptian pilots, supplemented by new recruits. As record numbers of ships passed through the Canal, the Egypt Committee accepted that Operation PILEUP was a failure.[13] Some frantic Ministers returned to the idea of collaboration with Israel. Lloyd eventually concluded that the effects 'would be deplorable and dangerous',[14] but at least two senior colleagues knew of an approach by Colonel Robert Henriques, a member of a prominent Anglo-Jewish family, to Israeli Prime Minister David Ben-Gurion.

8.6   1956   20 September
Message from Robert Henriques to Prime Minister Ben-Gurion

At all costs, Israel must avoid war with Jordan, but if, when Britain went into Suez, Israel were to attack simultaneously, it would be very convenient for all concerned. Britain would denounce Israel's aggression in the strongest possible terms, but at the peace negotiations afterwards, Britain would help Israel to get the best possible treaty.

Robert Henriques, 'The ultimatum: a dissenting view', *Spectator*, 6 November 1959, p. 623

Ben-Gurion just smiled and made no commitments.

On 19 September, the eighteen nations who approved the plans of the first London Conference reconvened to hear the report of the Menzies Mission and to consider their next step. With the Users Association already causing problems, Foster Dulles tried to reassure the British with his opening statement.

8.7   1956   19 September
Foster Dulles statement to the second London Conference of Maritime Nations

I do not care how many words are written into the Charter of the United Nations about not using force; if in fact there is not a

---

[13] Public Record Office, CAB134/1216, E.C.(56)29th meeting, 17 September 1956.
[14] Canadian National Archives, DEA 50372-40, Volume 4, London to Department of External Affairs, Cable 1200, 3 September 1956.

substitute for force, and some way of getting just solutions of some of these problems, inevitably the world will fall back again into anarchy and chaos.

Eisenhower Library, Eisenhower Papers, Ann Whitman Series, Dulles-Herter, Box 5, Cable DULTE 6, 20 September 1956

> The Secretary of State was bouncing back and forth dangerously. Days after telling a press conference that the Users Association would put no pressure upon Egypt, he was implying that a 'just solution' would be imposed upon Nasser if necessary. At the least, this indicated that the US would use the Association as an economic sanction, but Foster Dulles soon admitted to American journalists that 'the Users Association [was] not a device for denying Egypt any income at all with respect to the Canal'.[15] His hesitancy was reinforced by other countries who feared war with Egypt. Pakistan insisted that the Association's only purpose was negotiations with Nasser, and Scandinavian countries and Spain were close to rejecting any plan beyond the approval of discussions. When Japanese delegates pressed the Americans on the details of the Association, Foster Dulles admitted that he could not even force Egypt to accept the Assocation's pilots on ships transitting the Canal.[16] As the Conference finally agreed to form the Users Association, British Ministers were caught up in 'deepening depression'.

8.8   *1956   21 September*
Diary entry of William Clark, Press Secretary to Prime Minister Eden

A ghastly day with all the worst expectations turning up. Dulles pulled rug after rug from under us and watered down the Canal Users' Association until it was meaningless. . . . Pineau came in and seemed almost on the edge of dissolving the [Western] alliance.

William Clark Papers, File 7

> Publicly Britain and France accepted Dulles' diplomacy, but privately they were preparing to strike on their own. The British revived their plan of United Nations discussions as the pretext for military action

---

[15] US National Archives, Department of State, Central File, 974.7301/9-2056, London to State Department, Cable SECTO 20, 20 September 1956.

[16] See Lucas (1991, p. 207).

while the French pursued military planning with Israel. When Pineau asked the British to join the operations, Eden did not accept but he also indicated that Britain would not stop a Franco–Israeli attack upon Egypt.

8.9   1956   23 September
Account of Foreign Minister Pineau of meeting with Prime Minister Eden

Eden showed a good deal of interest; Lloyd a great deal of reticence. . . . Nevertheless I was able to persuade them to give me a kind of carte blanche to undertake further negotiations with the Israelis.

Cited in Terence Robertson, *Crisis: The Inside Story of the Suez Conspiracy*, London, 1965, p. 134

The turn of events offered a unique opportunity for Harold Macmillan, the Chancellor of the Exchequer. The leading advocate of co-operation with France and Israel, he was visiting the US in late September for talks with Eisenhower, with whom he had served in World War II, and Foster Dulles. Macmillan hoped that, even if the Americans did not join British plans, they would no longer delay them.

The outcome of Macmillan's mission is still one of the great curiosities of the crisis. His 35-minute visit with the President was an anticlimax. There was no direct reference to Suez although the Chancellor baffled Eisenhower with the assertion 'that, if it came to the worst, [Britain] would go down with the bands playing, the guns firing, and the flags flying'.[17] The conversation with Foster Dulles was clearer but no more helpful. The Secretary of State insisted he could not force ships to withhold dues from Egypt and warned that, if Nasser blocked the Canal, Britain would have to pay for oil from the Western Hemisphere. Macmillan admitted this was not possible, as 'the UK could not afford to borrow more dollars'. All Foster Dulles would offer was a return to the long-term proposals in OMEGA: 'The US Government was prepared to do everything it could to bring Nasser down, but . . . the most effective way of doing so was to let the present situation in the Canal continue and use other means of pressure which would shortly be discussed between us.'

---

[17] Eisenhower Library, Eisenhower Papers, Ann Whitman Series, DDE Diaries, Box 18, September 1956 Telephone Calls, Foster Dulles to Eisenhower, 25 September 1956.

8.10   *1956   25 September*
Record by Secretary of State Dulles of meeting with Chancellor of the Exchequer Macmillan

We discussed the plans for diminishing Nasser's prestige and I expressed the view that this could be done by economic and political means more effectively than by military means. Mr. Macmillan said to me the same thing that Anthony Eden had said on Thursday night, namely, that the present military situation was such that they could without undue expense hold action in abeyance.

Eisenhower Library, John Foster Dulles Papers, General Memoranda of Conversations, Box 1

> Incredibly, Macmillan never mentioned these clear warnings about the limits of American action to other Ministers. To the contrary, he wrote to Eden that Eisenhower was 'really determined, somehow or another, to bring Nasser down' and understood that Britain 'must win or the whole structure of our economy would collapse'. Foster Dulles also supposedly 'realised that [Britain] might have to act by force'. Macmillan concluded with the implication, disastrously wrong, that because of the Presidential election the US would not intervene against any military action before 6 November.

8.11   *1956   26 September*
Cable from Chancellor of the Exchequer Macmillan to Prime Minister Eden

[Secretary of State Dulles] quite realised that we might have to act by force. . . . Our threat of force was vital, whether we used it or not, to keep Nasser worried.

Public Record Office, PREM11/1102

> Given Macmillan's political experience, it is unlikely that he misunderstood the American sentiment against force. Instead, he judged that the risk of US opposition was not as great as that of British inaction.

8.12   *1956   4 October*
Diary entry by Chancellor of the Exchequer Macmillan

We must, by one means or another, win this struggle. Nasser may well try to preach Holy War in the Middle East and (even to

On the brink?

their own loss) the mob and the demagogues may create a ruinous position for us. Without oil, and without the profits from oil, neither UK nor Western Europe can survive.

Cited in Alistair Horne, *Macmillan: Volume I, 1894–1956*, London, 1986, p. 429

Macmillan's opinion was shared by the French leaders Mollet and Pineau, who met Eden and Lloyd in Paris on 26–27 September. The 'tough but uncompromising' position of the French impressed Eden, who saw 'the beginning of something like a renaissance of strength in France'.[18] Thus encouraged, the Prime Minister tested Eisenhower once more.

8.13   *1956   1 October*
Letter from Prime Minister Eden to President Eisenhower

There is no doubt in our minds that Nasser, whether he likes it or not, is now effectively in Russian hands, just as Mussolini was in Hitler's. It would be as ineffective to show weakness to Nasser now in order to placate him as it was to show weakness to Mussolini.

Public Record Office, PREM11/1177

Previously, Eisenhower and Dulles had always been careful to rule out the immediate use of force while assuring the British that something would be done with Nasser. The Secretary of State had been increasingly agitated, however, at his exclusion from the communication between Britain, France, and Israel. His response at a press conference on 2 October was hasty but decisive, killing off his own Users Association as a device for co-operation with Britain. He asserted, 'We are not now engaging in any economic war against Egypt' and repeated that 'there were never "teeth" in [the Association], if that means the use of force'. Instead of attacking Nasser, he turned on his 'allies' in Britain and France.

8.14   *1956   2 October*
Statement by Secretary of State Dulles at his press conference

I hope that we shall always stand together in treaty relations covering the North Atlantic, [but] any areas encroaching in some form or

[18] Cited in Gilbert (1988, p. 1214).

manner on the problem of so-called colonialism find the US playing a somewhat independent role.

Public Record Office, PREM11/1174, Washington to Foreign Office, Cable 2046, 2 October 1956

When Eden heard of Dulles' statement, he snapped at the Minister of State in the Foreign Office, Anthony Nutting, 'Now what have you to say for your American friends?'.[19] The angry Prime Minister now inspired comments in sympathetic newspapers.

8.15   1956   3 October
Leader in *The Times*

Mr Dulles's wavering course over the Suez issue has been watched in Britain with patient understanding because of the realisation that the US is on the eve of a presidential election and whatever he does or says has to pass the test of that scrutiny, but some of his words at yesterday's press conference can hardly claim the indulgence of that understanding any longer.

'Distorting the issues', *The Times*, 3 October 1956, p. 11

The following day, some Ministers asked the Cabinet to renew the commitment to force. They may even have requested approval for the alliance with Israel.[20] Apparently, the Eden Government was ready to act without Washington's consent.

---

[19] Nutting (1967, p. 70).
[20] Public Record Office, CAB128/130, C.M.68(56), 3 October 1956; Hugh Thomas (1966, p. 96).

9

Force dismissed

As in late August, Britain was on the brink of war, but facing the abyss, it pulled back. The chief waverer was Foreign Secretary Lloyd, who was considering the plan of Indian Foreign Minister Krishna Menon for a system of guarantees between the Egyptian Canal Authority and the Users Association over development of the Canal and transit dues. Others on the Egypt Committee admitted that the arrangements for consultation were 'probably more satisfactory than any proposal that could be agreed with Egypt after the expiration of the original concession [to the Suez Canal Company] in 1968'.[1] The appeal to the UN Security Council, which was supposed to prepare for war, now played into the hands of the peacemakers, as Foreign Office officials who were sceptical about force took over the talks. Their position was reinforced by Foster Dulles.

9.1 *1956 5 October*
Statement by Secretary of State Dulles to Foreign Secretary Lloyd and Foreign Minister Pineau

Sometimes one must use [force] without prospect of a satisfactory outcome, but force is not a measure which will improve our prospects in Asia and Africa, and it is a great illusion to think that it would. . . .

The use of force in violation of the Charter would destroy the United Nations. That is a grave responsibility.

US National Archives, Department of State, Central File, 974.7301/10–656, New York to State Department, Cable DULTE 1, 5 October 1956

[1] Public Record Office, CAB134/1216, E.C.(56)31st meeting, 25 September 1956.

With Eden in the hospital with a high fever, Macmillan tried to rally the Egypt Committee, which instructed Lloyd to insist upon the eighteen-power plan and to press the US to pay all Canal dues to the Users Association.[2] Events in New York were moving too fast for the 'hawks', however, as the Security Council adjourned for Lloyd and Pineau to negotiate privately with Egyptian Foreign Minister Mahmoud Fawzi.[3]

Neither the Egypt Committee nor Eden, upon his return from hospital, could halt the talks, since this would put Britain in the wrong before world opinion and ruin any pretext for force. The Prime Minister instructed Lloyd to 'spin out' the discussions while the Americans were urged to reconsider economic sanctions against Egypt, but the strategy was ruined when Fawzi made concessions to the British, notably that Egyptian politics would not be allowed to interfere with the Canal's operation.[4]

By 11 October, the Egypt Committee conceded, 'The present proposals would at least provide a system of international cooperation with a considerable amount of financial control.' Eden cabled Lloyd that he was 'delighted to see that [Lloyd] fought so hard' in the discussions for a satisfactory settlement.[5]

9.2   1956   11 October
Comments by Prime Minister Eden to Ministers

The Foreign Secretary should be told that, provided the present pressure was maintained on the Egyptian representatives in these negotiations, he should not feel himself bound to terminate the discussions by the end of this week if at the time it appeared that a satisfactory agreement would shortly be obtained.

Public Record Office, PREM11/1102

The chief barrier to peace was no longer Britain but France. Lloyd informed Eden that Pineau was 'determined (a) to prevent any agreement, (b) to present our negotiations in the worst possible light, (c) to

[2] Public Record Office, CAB134/1216, E.C.(56)33rd meeting, 8 October 1956.
[3] Public Record Office, PREM11/1102, New York to Foreign Office, Cable 814, 9 October 1956.
[4] Public Record Office, CAB134/1216, E.C.(56)34th meeting, 10 October 1956; Public Record Office, PREM11/1102, New York to Foreign Office, Cables 819 and 821, 10–11 October 1956.
[5] Public Record Office, PREM11/1102, Ministerial meeting, 11 October 1956, and Foreign Office to New York, Cable 1125, 11 October 1956.

end up with an expression of opinion by the Security Council which would tie our hands'.[6] Undeterred, Lloyd and Fawzi agreed on 'Six Principles' for the Canal, including 'free and open transit through the Canal' and 'respect for Egyptian sovereignty'. The Security Council adopted the Six Principles on 14 October, although the question of how to implement those Principles remained open. Lloyd, realising that Pineau would not stay in New York beyond 14 October, agreed with the French to introduce the eighteen-power plan of international control. The Security Council voted nine to two for the Plan, but the veto of the Soviet Union prevented its passage.[7]

Lloyd concluded to Eden that the option of military action was still available, but only if Egypt refused to continue discussions.

9.3   1956   14 October
Cable from Foreign Secretary Lloyd to Prime Minister Eden

We emerge without any result enjoining us against force or to set up a negotiating committee. . . . With the changed atmosphere here, we can count on a more understanding reaction if we have to take extreme measures. . . . [However] we are now committed to further exchanges with Egypt without a time limit.

Public Record Office, PREM11/1102, New York to Foreign Office, Cable 854, 14 October 1956

The Prime Minister was at his country home, Chequers, on Sunday morning, 14 October, with Lloyd's deputy, Anthony Nutting, when the final report arrived from New York. Eden had told the Conservative Party Conference the previous day, 'We have refused to say that in no circumstances would we ever use force',[8] but his resolve for an assault had disappeared. A reply to Lloyd, drafted by Nutting and approved by Eden, laid out the path for further negotiations.

9.4   1956   14 October
Cable from Prime Minister Eden to Foreign Secretary Lloyd

Should not we and the French now approach the Egyptians and ask them whether they are prepared to meet and discuss in confidence

[6] Public Record Office, PREM11/1102, New York to Foreign Office, Cable 829, 11 October 1956.
[7] Public Record Office, PREM11/1102, New York to Foreign Office, Cable 854, 14 October 1956.
[8] Eden (1960, p. 507).

with us on the basis of the second half of the resolution which the Russians vetoed? If they say yes, then it is for consideration whether we and the French meet them somewhere, e.g. Geneva. If they say no, then they will be in defiance of the view of nine members of the Security Council and a new situation will arise.

Public Record Office, PREM11/1102, Foreign Office to New York, Cable 1198, 14 October 1956

> The decision was confirmed by changes in British military plans. Because of the winter weather in the Mediterranean, Operation REVISE for bombing and psychological warfare, followed by landings in the Canal Zone, could not be maintained after late October. The British Chiefs of Staff replaced REVISE with a 'Winter Plan' in which any ground operations would be delayed until spring 1957. The new plan would take effect on 19 October.[9]
>
> The Suez Crisis was almost over. The Americans were not directly responsible, but the sustained pressure by Washington had delayed Britain long enough for other influences, such as the caution of the Foreign Office and the restrictions on the military timetable, to take effect.

9.5   1956   12 October
Statement by President Eisenhower at his press conference

It looks like here is a very crisis that is behind us. I do not mean to say that we are completely out of the woods, but I talked to the Secretary of State just before I came over here tonight and I will tell you [that] in both his heart and mine there is a very great prayer of thanksgiving.

Cited in Selwyn Lloyd, *Suez 1956*, New York, 1978, p. 160

---

[9] Public Record Office, PREM11/1104, COS(56)380, 'Operation MUSKETEER: Winter Plan', 12 October 1956.

10

Force resurrected

At 1.30 p.m. on 14 October, Eden's telegram proposing negotiations with the Egyptians in Geneva was despatched to Lloyd. At 3 p.m., the Prime Minister received two French envoys, Acting Foreign Minister Albert Gazier and General Maurice Challe, at Chequers. An hour later, Eden's telegram to Lloyd was out-of-date: the Anglo-French military option has been revived and the idea of working with the Israelis had been approved by both sides.

Eden, hiding the collusion with Israel, never referred to the encounter in his memoirs, but in 1967 Anthony Nutting, the Foreign Office Minister of State who was present at the meeting, gave a detailed account.

10.1 *1956   14 October*
Recollection of Minister of State Anthony Nutting of meeting between Prime Minister Eden and two French representatives

Gazier then proceeded to ask us what would be Britain's reaction if Israel were to attack Egypt. Eden replied that this was a very difficult question. The Tripartite Declaration [of 1950] would presumably be invoked, and this would involve us as signatories.

'But would you resist Israel by force of arms?' Gazier asked. To this Eden replied with a half-laugh that he could hardly see himself fighting for Colonel Nasser! Then, casting his mind back to the 1954 agreement about the Suez base, he turned to me and said, 'Didn't your agreement say something about our not being obliged to send troops if Egypt was attacked by Israel?'

I replied that . . . this provision only governed our rights to return to the base and did not in any way nullify our obligations under the Tripartite Declaration to resist any attack across the armistice borders of Israel and the Arab world. We had reaffirmed these obligations publicly on countless occasions before and since the 1954 agreement had been signed, and there was no getting away from them.

Eden looked somewhat crestfallen at this. But a moment later he could scarcely contain his glee when Glazier reminded him that the Egyptians had recently contended that the Tripartite Declaration did not apply to Egypt. . . .

'So that lets us off the hook,' Eden said excitedly, 'We have no obligation, it seems, to stop the Israelis attacking the Egyptians.' [. . .]

Challe then proceeded to outline what he termed a possible plan of action for Britain and France to gain physical control of the Suez Canal. The plan, as he put it to us, was that Israel should be invited to attack Egypt across the Sinai Peninsula and that France and Britain, having given the Israeli forces enough time to seize all or most of Sinai, should then order 'both sides' to withdraw their forces from the Suez Canal, in order to permit an Anglo–French force to intervene and occupy the Canal on the pretext of saving it from damage by fighting.

Anthony Nutting, *No End of a Lesson*, London, 1967, pp. 91–3

The encounter has been regarded by most historians as the key moment leading to the Suez War. Yet it is still unclear *why* Eden accepted the French proposals. The standard explanation is that Eden, with his hatred of Nasser and fear of the Egyptian threat, was just looking for an excuse to renew military preparation. This is insufficient. British Ministers, despite their anger, had consistently rejected the option of working with Israel, and Eden himself had rebuked Macmillan for the idea in August and declined another French approach in late September. Why then pursue collusion in October?

Part of the answer could be sheer desperation by Eden, since his options for the use of force had been exhausted by 14 October. Yet another part lies in a far different explanation, mentioned by Nutting but generally ignored by historians. In effect, the French blackmailed the British. They warned that, if Britain did not join France and Israel, there would be an Israeli attack upon Jordan, her neighbour to the east. With France supporting the Israelis, the British would be left with a terrible choice: either they abandoned Jordan and lost their Middle Eastern position or they entered a war against France and Israel.

Killings on the Israeli–Jordanian border, which had threatened war in July, had resumed in September. With a special Israeli military unit retaliating for attacks upon soldiers and border guards, thirty-nine troops and civilians were slain in two weeks. Jordan's King Hussein asked Iraq to send a division of troops to protect against a full-scale Israeli attack.[1]

These developments were both unexpected opportunity and danger for Britain. Ever since the decision to remove British troops from the Suez Canal Base, London's political and military strategy relied upon treaties with Iraq and Jordan. After Jordan's dismissal in March 1956 of General Glubb, the British commander of its army, the Eden Government had encouraged Iraqi–Jordanian contacts to fill the vacuum. Thus, any deployment of Iraqi soldiers inside Jordan would be a permanent commitment to Arab defence in partnership with Britain. On the other hand, Israel and Iraq had never signed a peace treaty after the Arab–Israeli War of 1948–49, and the Israeli Government of David Ben-Gurion might react violently to the stationing of Iraqi troops on its border.

The Eden Government decided to stand by the Iraqi–Jordanian axis while informing Israel about the nature of the deployment.

10.2   *1956   1 October*
Egypt Committee meeting

The Foreign Secretary . . . suggested that the Israeli Government should again be warned that, in the event of their attacking Jordan, we should honour our obligation under the Anglo/Jordan Treaty to go to Jordan's assistance. This warning could be linked to the recent Israeli raids against Jordan territory. However it was already the intention to inform the Israeli Government, if agreement was reached between Jordan and Iraq to send an Iraqi brigade to Jordan.

Public Record Office, CAB134/1216, EC(56)32nd meeting

> At first, the strategy was successful. Iraq and Jordan were reassured by offers of military equipment and British air and naval support, while Ben-Gurion told the US Ambassador to Israel that he would not object if no 'unreasonably large number' of Iraqi soldiers entered Jordan and if none of them were placed on the west bank of the Jordan River next to Israel.[2]

[1] See Lucas (1991, pp. 228–9).
[2] US National Archives, Department of State, Central File, 684A.85/10-656, Tel Aviv to State Deparment, Cable 310, 3 October 1956.

Unfortunately, a diplomatic mix-up led to a critical delay in obtaining Ben-Gurion's final agreement. In the interim, vehement Israeli opponents of the move, notably Foreign Minister Golda Meir and the Chief of Staff of the military, General Moshe Dayan, hastened to prevent it once and for all. Their hand was strengthened when the Iraqi Prime Minister Nuri Sa'id unwisely told *The Times* that Israel should return some territory to the Arabs in exchange for a final peace agreement.

10.3 *1956* *9 October*
Foreign Minister Meir to US Ambassador Lawson

Israel will not sit by while these events develop. We will not make it so comfortable for them. We are not going to be destroyed without a struggle.

US National Archives, Department of State, Central File, 684A.85/10-956, Tel Aviv to State Department, Cable 340

At 11:55 p.m. on 10 October, an Israeli division of troops attacked the Jordanian border on a twelve-mile front centred upon the village of Qalqilya. More than seventy Jordanians were killed and more than forty wounded, and the Israeli Defence Forces lost eighteen men, an unusually high total for a 'reprisal' raid. At one point, Israeli troops were five miles inside Jordan and American observers feared that war had begun.[3]

The Israeli Government officially claimed that Qalqilya was a 'hastily planned, organised, and carried out' reprisal for the murder of two Israeli farm labourers,[4] but this was belied by the size of the raid and the days of penetration it required. A more obvious link was between the raid and the Israeli warning to Britain and Jordan to halt the deployment of Iraqi forces. The day after Qalqilya, the Israeli Government publicly stated, '[Iraqi] action would be a direct threat to the security of Israel and to the validity of the Israeli–Jordanian armistice agreement.'[5]

[3] US National Archives, Records of the Joint Chiefs of Staff, Geographical File, 1954–6, Box 14, S. 42, Collins to Radford, 11 October 1956.
[4] See Dayan (1976, p. 172).
[5] Public Record Office, FO371/121780/VR1091/310, Tel Aviv to Foreign Office, Cable 491, 12 October 1956.

10.4   *1956*   15 October
Report from a 'reliable informant' to the British Consulate, Jerusalem

The [Israeli] Cabinet was influenced by the information that [Meir] had obtained . . . about the number of Iraqi troops and their length of stay in Jordan . . . Israel intended to take part of West Bank from Ramallah to Nalbus and the North.

Public Record Office, FO371/121781/VR1091/320, Jerusalem to Foreign Office, Cable 385

Israel had assumed a great risk with Qalqilya. Despite the demands of the Suez crisis, the British military plan to bomb the Israeli Air Force and blockade the Israeli coast, codenamed CORDAGE, was operational. Hours before Qalqilya, the British Chiefs of Staff put to Ministers the choice of preparing for war with Egypt or war with Israel.

10.5   *1956*   10 October
British Chiefs of Staff assessment

[We] should bring home very forcibly to Ministers that we could either go to the aid of Jordan against Israel with sea and air power, or we could launch MUSKETEER [REVISE]; we could not do both.

Public Record Office, DEFE4/91, COS(56)98th meeting, 10 October 1956

Why then did Israel proceed, only months after Ben-Gurion had told the Israeli Parliament, 'I will never send Israeli defence forces to fight any European, American, British, Russian or French army'?[6]

The probable answer is that the Qalqilya raid had a second objective: to prepare for war against Egypt. According to a top-secret military plan, codenamed ESAU, troops would be concentrated in north and central Israel to draw attention from mobilisation on the Egyptian border. This phase was to begin ten days before the Franco–Israeli invasion of Egypt on 20 October. Thus Qalqilya would have been ESAU's first operation.

[6] Public Record Office, FO371/121728/VR1073/185, Chancery (Tel Aviv) to Levant Department, 21 June 1956.

10.6
Description by Israeli historian Yigal Sheffy of Operation ESAU

The deception story, which was to provide support for the possibility of an attack on Jordan and obscure the Egyptian option, entailed initiation of activity along the Jordanian border. . . . The beginning of this phase was set for D-Day minus ten days, perhaps because it was believed that this was the time necessary for the deception story to sink in.

Yigal Sheffy, 'Unconcern at dawn, surprise at sunset: Egyptian intelligence appreciations before the Sinai campaign, 1956', *Intelligence and National Security*, July 1990, p. 34

It is also possible that Qalqilya had the third purpose of scaring the British into joining the Franco–Israeli attack. The original plan for an invasion on 20 October had encountered unexpected opposition from Ben-Gurion. The Prime Minister, fearing Egyptian bombing of Israeli cities, would only accept the plan if British bombers knocked out the Egyptian Air Force. Ben-Gurion believed that there was only a twenty per cent chance that London would accept such a role, but French Foreign Minister Pineau held out hope that the British would co-operate to avoid war over Jordan.[7] According to Pineau, Eden, referring to the Israeli–Jordanian tension, had announced, 'What a pity that these incidents [are] not taking place on the Egyptian border!'[8] After a meeting with Ben-Gurion and French representatives, the Israeli military leader Moshe Dayan noted cryptically, 'If the thing [the Franco–Israeli operation] is postponed at present, it might be that something will be cooked up in France and Jordan.'[9] The content of Dayan's talks with his French counterparts, one of whom was the same Maurice Challe who met Eden on 14 October, is unknown, but General André Beaufre, the commander of French land forces for REVISE, later wrote, 'It seems that the [French] Colonial Office tried some complicated manoeuvre in Jordan to incite Nasser to attack Israel and so provide justification for our operations.'[10]

The exact purpose of the Qalqilya raid is probably hidden in classified French and Israeli documents. However, what is certain is that Gazier and Challe began their meeting with Eden with a discussion of Jordan. Gazier appealed to Eden to stop the Iraqi deployment and

[7] See Dayan (1976, p. 166).
[8] Cited in Abel Thomas (1978, p. 150)
[9] Ben-Gurion Archives, Ben-Gurion diary entry, 3 October 1956.
[10] Beaufre (1969, p. 77).

asked the Prime Minister whether Britain wanted to provoke Israel further. When Nutting replied that it was Britain's idea to move the troops, Eden cut him short and said that he would ask the Iraqis to suspend the deployment temporarily. Only then did Gazier ask about the British reaction to an Israeli attack upon Egypt.[11]

[11] Public Record Office, FO371/121488/VJ10393/134, Foreign Office to Baghdad, Cable 2152, 14 October 1956.

11

From collusion to war

Despite Eden's apparent change of heart, a British attack with France and Israel was far from a certainty. The Prime Minister allowed Nutting to inform two Foreign Office personnel of events, although Eden had objected to consultation with the Foreign Office Legal Adviser because 'the lawyers are always against our doing anything'. Nutting and the officials agreed that the French plan was disastrous: Lloyd's work at the United Nations would be undone, the US would be angered, the Commonwealth would be divided, and the stability of the pro-Western Arab regimes would be endangered.[1]

Eden cleared this hurdle easily, rejecting the brief out of hand and winning the approval on 16 October of other Ministers, except for Minister of Defence Monckton, for the Gazier–Challe proposal. His next obstacle might have been Lloyd, who returned from New York and told Nutting, 'We must have nothing to do with the French plan.'[2] The Foreign Secretary withheld his objections in the Ministerial meeting, however, and agreed to accompany Eden to Paris that afternoon.

11.1
Recollection of Anthony Nutting, Minister of State in the Foreign Office in 1956

Eden had clearly used the lunch interval to devastating effect, for Lloyd not only seemed prepared to acquiesce in the French plan but now took the line that his agreement with [Egyptian Foreign Minister] Fawzi would never hold. . . . Echoing Eden, he kept

[1] See Nutting (1967, p. 95).
[2] Cited in Nutting (1967, p. 97).

repeating that we could not trust Nasser to honour any commitment.

Anthony Nutting, *No End of a Lesson*, London, 1967, p. 98

In the discussions with Mollet and Pineau, Lloyd made a final attempt to save the negotiations with Egypt for some form of 'international control' of the Canal, but the French leaders bluntly called this 'quite unsatisfactory'. Eden now took over. He agreed with Mollet and Pineau that the UN was not an obstacle since 'it was not thought likely that the Security Council would reach agreement on any action taken'. He also repeated 'that, if Israel were to act before the end of the American election campaign', the US would be unable to intervene with military forces against Britain and France. (Significantly, Eden never considered if the US would resort to diplomatic or economic pressure, rather than military action, to stop the war.) Mollet then established the pretext for British involvement.

11.2   *1956   16 October*
Record of Foreign Secretary Lloyd of Anglo-French meeting

MOLLET: If Israel attacked Egypt, would UK feel bound to intervene under the Tripartite Declaration?
EDEN: He thought the answer to that would be 'no' but he would confirm that to M. Mollet after he got back to London.
MOLLET: In the event of the likelihood of hostilities in the vicinity of the Canal, would the UK Government intervene to stop them?
EDEN: He thought the answer to that question would be 'yes'.

Public Record Office, FO800/725, Lloyd minute, 18 October 1956

Now the task was to bring the British together with the Israelis. Ben-Gurion was sceptical, since Britain and France would not attack Egypt simultaneously with Israel but would only occupy the Suez Canal Zone *after* Israel had invaded the Sinai Desert in eastern Egypt. He wrote, 'The British plot, I imagine, is to get us involved with Nasser and bring about the occupation of Jordan by Iraq.' However, Ben-Gurion confirmed that 'the representatives of Israel [were] ready to come immediately in utmost secrecy' to discussions.[3] For his part, Eden suspended

---

[3] See Bar-Zohar (1967, p. 234); Mordechai Bar-On, 'David Ben-Gurion and the Sèvres Collusion' in Louis and Owen (1989, p. 149); Troen and Shemesh (1990), p. 302.

the Iraqi deployment permanently and stood down the Royal Air Force, which had been on alert to defend Jordan against Israel.[4]

The first meeting between Britain, France, and Israel was held on 22 October at Sèvres outside Paris. It did not begin well. Lloyd, still unhappy about collusion, was shaken on the trip from the French air-field to Sèvres when his automobile was nearly hit by a speeding car. According to French officials, the serious tone of the occasion was further undermined by the false moustache that Lloyd was wearing.[5] Whether or not the Foreign Secretary was in disguise, an Israeli repre-sentative was less than flattering about the initial talks.

11.3   1956   22 October
Account by Mordechai Bar-On, assistant to Prime Minister Ben-Gurion, of Sèvres meeting

[Lloyd's] voice was shrill and started with an unpleasant tone of cyn-icism and a humour dry as a clay shard. His face gave the impression of something stinking hanging permanently under his nose. The snobbish air of his entire personality prevented him from opening himself up to his fellow negotiators and shed on the entire conversa-tion a cold and formal atmosphere.

Mordechai Bar-On, 'David Ben-Gurion and the Sèvres Collusion', in W. R. Louis and Roger Owen (eds.), *Suez 1956: The Crisis and its Consequences*, Oxford: Clarendon, 1989, p. 157

The crisis again arose over the timing of the British intervention. Lloyd repeated that, if Israel attacked Egypt *alone*, Britain and France would safeguard the Suez Canal on the pretext of stopping the fight. He refused to reduce the 48-hour gap between the Israeli invasion and British bombing of Egypt. He also rejected compromise proposals, such as the loan of British bombers to the French, who could use them to assist the Israelis. A furious Ben-Gurion believed that Britain, to maintain the illusion that they were peacekeepers rathers than allies of France and Israel, were leaving his country at the mercy of the Egyptian Air Force.[6]

---

[4] See Lucas (1991, pp. 242–3).
[5] BBC television production, *Secrets of Suez* (1986) interview with Maurice Bourges-Maunoury.
[6] See Lucas (1991, pp. 244–5).

11.4 *1956   23 October*
Statement by Prime Minister Eden at Cabinet meeting

From secret conversations which had been held in Paris with representatives of the Israeli Government, it now appeared that the Israelis would not alone launch a full-scale attack against Egypt. The United Kingdom were thus confronted with the choice between an early military operation or a relatively prolonged negotiation.

Public Record Office, CAB128/30, C.M.72(56)

The French had not given up, however, and after lengthy discussions on 23 October, the Israeli military leader Moshe Dayan found the solution. Israeli paratroopers would launch a surprise attack on the Mitla Pass, seventy miles inside Egypt and thirty miles from the Suez Canal, while armed columns moved into the Sinai desert. Britain and France would launch their air strikes thirty-six hours later. Dayan was gambling that the Egyptians, believing the attack on the Mitla Pass was only a raid, would not send their bombers against Israel. Ben-Gurion agreed that Pineau could take the plan to London that evening.[7]

When Pineau arrived, Lloyd tried to describe the advantages of a UN solution, but he gave way when Eden joined the meeting. The Prime Minister and Pineau decided that they 'might serve notice on the parties to stop and withdraw a certain distance from the Canal and threaten them with military intervention by France and Britain if that was not done'.[8] Reassured, Eden hinted to the Cabinet the next morning:

11.5 *1956   24 October*
Statement by Prime Minister Eden to Cabinet meeting

If [an Anglo-French operation] were launched, Israel would make a full-scale attack against Egypt, and this might have the effect of reducing the period of preliminary [aerial] bombardment. The second objective of the operation would be to secure the downfall of Colonel Nasser's regime in Egypt.

Was it not likely that such an operation would unite the Arab world in support of Egypt? The Prime Minister said that this was a serious risk; but against it must be set the greater risk that, unless early action could be taken to damage Colonel Nasser's prestige, his

[7] See Lucas (1991, pp. 246–7).
[8] Public Record Office, FO800/725, Lloyd minute, 24 October 1956.

influence would be extended throughout the Middle East to a degree which would make it much more difficult to overthrow him. It was known that [Nasser] was already plotting *coups* in many of the other Arab countries; and we should never have a better pretext for intervention against him than we had now as a result of his seizure of the Suez Canal.

Public Record Office, CAB128/30, C.M.73(56)

> With Lloyd speaking in the House of Commons that afternoon, Eden instructed two Foreign Office officials, Patrick Dean and Donald Logan, to return to Sèvres.
> The second set of Sèvres talks were anticlimactic, since Pineau had agreed the main points with the Israelis and Eden before Dean and Logan arrived. The 'Sèvres Protocol' recorded that Israel would launch 'a full-scale attack' on the afternoon of 29 October. The next day, the British and French Governments would demand that Egypt and Israel cease fire and withdraw ten miles either side of the Suez Canal while Anglo–French forces established a 'temporary occupation of the key positions on the Canal'. The inevitable Egyptian refusal of the ultimatum would bring British and French bombing 'early on October 31st'.[9]
> The Sèvres meetings had a farcical postscript. When Eden learned that collusion had been recorded in the Sèvres Protocol, he instructed Dean and Logan to return to Paris to destroy all copies of the document. The unfortunate envoys were left in a locked room for hours, without food or drink, while Pineau phoned the Israelis. Ben-Gurion, fearing that the British would abandon the agreement, refused Eden's request.[10]
> The Prime Minister was more successful with his Cabinet, although it is still unclear if he revealed the collusion with Israel.

11.6   1956   25 October
Statement by Prime Minister Eden to Cabinet

The French Government were strongly of the view that intervention would be justified in order to limit [Egyptian–Israeli] hostilities and that for this purpose it would be right to launch the military operation against Egypt which had already been mounted.

Public Record Office, CAB128/30, C.M.74(56)

[9] See Bar-Zohar (1967, p. 246); Dayan (1976, p. 191).
[10] Liddell Hart Centre for Military Archives, Suez Oral History Project, interview with Donald Logan.

Walter Monckton, soon to resign as Minister of Defence, and some junior Ministers argued that an ultimatum to Egypt and Israel to keep their troops ten miles from the Suez Canal would 'not appear to be holding the balance' since it would allow Israel to establish a line ninety miles inside Egypt. The UN might object, and 'our action would cause offence to the US Government and might do lasting damage to Anglo–American relations'. However, most of the Cabinet supported Eden on the flimsy pretext that 'we should be intervening to prevent interference with the free flow of traffic through the Canal' or the rationalisation that 'a crisis in the Middle East could not now be long delayed'. As one Minister recalled, 'We were offered the poisoned chalice, we had the choice of draining it to the bitter dregs or dashing it from our lips.'[11]

Eden did not even tell his military leaders of the details of the collusion. When the Commander-in-Chief of REVISE, General Charles Keightley, expressed anxiety about operations, 'Eden gave him a severe dressing down and told him that these were questions with which military commanders should not concern themselves'.[12] British forces only prepared for invasion when the commander of land forces, General Hugh Stockwell, was told by his French counterpart 'that the Israelis were going to attack Egypt and that we would undoubtedly get involved'. REVISE's air commander, Air Marshal Denis Barnett, learned of the change in plans when a note was blown off Keightley's desk onto the floor: 'Hooknoses D-Day 29 Oct.'[13]

The Eisenhower Administration first suspected something was wrong when the US Embassy in London could not provide an account of the Anglo-French meeting of 16 October. Concern increased when a French Minister, Jacques Chaban-Delmas, told the US Ambassador to France that Britain, France, and Israel were planning to attack Israel about 10 November. The U-2, America's new spy plane, photographed the movement of Israeli troops and the sailing of British and French convoys to the Eastern Mediterranean. Yet the Americans still saw 'Jordan as the most probable direction' for an Israeli attack.[14] Lloyd muddied the waters further by lying to the US Ambassador in London.

---

[11] Hugh Thomas (1966, p. 182).
[12] Cited in Bernard Levin, *The Times*, 11 November 1980.
[13] BBC radio broadcast, *A Canal Too Far*, 1987, interviews with Kenneth Darling and Denis Barnett.
[14] See Lucas (1991, pp. 253–5).

11.7 *1956 29 October*
Cable from Winthrop Aldrich, the U.S. Ambassador in London, to State Department

[Lloyd] was unwilling to believe the Israelis would launch a full-scale attack upon Egypt despite the temptation to do so in the present circumstances. He also said categorically that his recent conversations with the French gave him no reason to think the French were stimulating such an Israeli venture.

US National Archives, Department of State, Central File, 684A.86/10–2956, London to State Department, Cable 2322

12

Anatomy of failure

At 5 p.m., Cairo time, on 29 October, four low-flying Israeli planes cut
Egyptian phone lines as 395 paratroopers dropped into the Mitla Pass.
Because of the collusion, Britain's diplomatic and military forces were
unprepared. When the British Ambassador in Israel approached Ben-
Gurion because Britain 'hoped no further action is contemplated
against Jordan', the Israeli Prime Minister replied curtly, 'I think you
will find your government knows more about this than you do.'[1] The
situation was even worse in Washington: the new British Ambassador
was not leaving London for the United States until 1 November (and
then by ship rather than plane) and the Acting Ambassador, John
Coulson, was not given any instructions by London for more than two
hours after the Israeli attack.[2]

The assumption of Eden and Macmillan that the Americans would
not intervene was shattered immediately, as Eisenhower berated
Coulson.

12.1 *1956 29 October*
Record of meeting between President Eisenhower and John Coulson, British Chargé d'Affaires in Washington

The President [said] that the prestige of the United States and the
British is involved in the developments in the Middle East. He felt it
was incumbent upon both of us to redeem our word about supporting any victim of aggression. . . . 'We plan to get [to the United

[1] Public Record Office, FO371/121782/VR1091/368, Foreign Office to Tel Aviv,
Cable 1025, 17 October 1956.
[2] Public Record Office, FO371/121763/VR1076/122, Foreign Office to Washington,
Cable 4987, 29 October 1956.

Nations Security Council] the first thing in the morning – when the doors open – before the USSR gets there.'

Eisenhower Library, Eisenhower Papers, Ann Whitman Series, DDE Diaries, Box, 19, October 1956, Staff Memoranda, Goodpaster memorandum

> The British and American delegations at the United Nations were already feuding.

12.2   *1956   29 October*
Telephone call from Secretary of State Dulles to Henry Cabot Lodge, US Ambassador to the United Nations

Ambassador Lodge . . . said he had just talked to Sir Pierson Dixon [British Ambassador to the United Nations]. He said it was one of the most disagreeable and unpleasant experiences that he had ever had. He said that Dixon until now had always been amiable but at this conference the mask fell off and he was virtually snarling. When Lodge had spoken of living up to the Tripartite Declaration [to stop the Israeli aggression against Egypt], Dixon had said, 'Don't be silly and moralistic. We have got to be practical.' Dixon said that the British would never go along with any move against Israel in the Security Council.

Eisenhower Library, John Foster Dulles Papers, Telephone Calls, Box 5

> The British Cabinet, pressed by Lloyd, suddenly recognised, 'Our reserves of gold and dollars [are] still in need of assistance, and we [can]not afford to alienate the US Government more than [is] absolutely necessary.'[3] So Eden cabled Eisenhower on 30 October that, while 'Egypt had to a large extent brought this attack on herself', Britain's intervention was to defend access through the Suez Canal.

12.3   *1956   30 October*
Letter from Prime Minister Eden to President Eisenhower

We have earnestly deliberated what we should do in this serious situation. We cannot afford to see the Canal closed or to lose the

---

[3] Public Record Office, CAB134/1216, C.M.75(56), 30 October 1956.

shipping which is daily on passage through it. . . . We feel that decisive action should be taken at once to stop hostilities.

Public Record Office, PREM11/1177, Foreign Office to Washington, Cable 5010, 30 October 1956

> The President was not convinced, for the British continued to block any Security Council resolution that condemned Israel. He complained about his 'unworthy and unreliable ally' and concluded, 'We will not help them.'[4]
> Eden persisted in his foolish charade. He informed the House of Commons at 4:30 p.m. on the 30th of the Anglo-French demand that Egypt and Israel withdraw ten miles from the Suez Canal and allow British and French forces into the Canal Zone.

12.4 *1956 30 October*
Statement by Prime Minister Eden to the House of Commons

As a result of the consultations held in London today, the United Kingdom and French Governments have now addressed urgent communications to the Governments of Egypt and Israel. In these we have called upon both sides to stop all warlike action by land, sea and air forthwith and to withdraw their military forces to a distance of 10 miles from the Canal. Further, in order to separate the belligerents and to guarantee freedom of transit through the Canal by the ships of all nations, we have asked the Egyptian Government to agree that Anglo–French forces should move temporarily – I repeat, temporarily – into key positions at Port Said, Ismailia, and Suez.

The Governments of Egypt and Israel have been asked to answer this communication within twelve hours. It has been made clear to them that, if at the expiration of that time one or both have not undertaken to comply with these requirements, British and French forces will intervene in whatever strength may be necessary to secure compliance.

Hansard, House of Commons, 30 October 1956, Vol. 558, Col. 1275

> Since the main Israeli force was still far from the Canal, the Israelis could advance forty to ninety miles inside Egypt and comply with the

---

[4] Eisenhower Library, John Foster Dulles Papers, Telephone Calls, White House, Box 10, Foster Dulles to Eisenhower, 30 October 1956.

'impartial' British ultimatum. Given only fifteen minutes' notice of Eden's announcement, the Labour leader Hugh Gaitskell exclaimed, 'I shall never believe anything that Eden says to me in public or in private.'[5] However, Gaitskell knew more than Eisenhower and Foster Dulles, who only received Eden's explanation of the ultimatum four hours after the speech in the Commons. The story that Eisenhower phoned Eden with a stream of expletives and 'Anthony, you must have gone out of your mind', only to realise that he had been connected to Eden's Press Secretary by mistake, may not be true,[6] but the President and Foster Dulles had no intention of being pulled along by the British.

12.5 1956 31 October
Statement by Secretary of State Dulles to Vice President Nixon

Two things are important from this standpoint of history. It is the beginning of the collapse of the Soviet Empire [because of the Hungarian uprising]. The second is the idea is out that we can be dragged along at the heels of British and French policies that are obsolete. This is a declaration of independence for the first time that they cannot count upon us to engage in policies of this sort.

Eisenhower Library, John Foster Dulles Papers, Telephone Calls, Box 5, Nixon to Foster Dulles, 31 October 1956

Still, despite the diplomatic disaster caused by the ultimatum, Britain might have succeeded if it had occupied the Suez Canal Zone quickly, provoking the Egyptians to overthrow Nasser. After considering the British ultimatum to Egypt, Eisenhower drafted a message to Eden.

12.6 1956 30 October
Draft message from President Eisenhower to Prime Minister Eden

I think I faintly understand and certainly I deeply sympathize with you in the problem you have to solve. Now we must pray that everything comes out both justly and reasonably peacefully.

Eisenhower Library, Eisenhower Papers, Ann Whitman Series, Dulles-Herter, Box 5, October 1956 (1)

[5] Liddell Hart Centre for Military Archives, Suez Oral History Project, interview with Douglas Jay.
[6] BBC radio broadcast, *Neither War nor Peace at 10 Downing Street* (1979) interview with William Clark.

The President delayed sending the message to await further event, but American ambivalence continued. US spy planes, passing over damaged Egyptian airfields, sent their photographs to British analysts, and the CIA continued to liaise with MI6.

12.7 1964 28 July
Recollection by President Eisenhower

Had they done it quickly, we would have accepted it. . . . They could have taken over and then got out of there. There'd have been no great crisis in the world.

Eisenhower Library, Eisenhower Papers, Oral History Collection, OH-14

Thus the critical British failure was the inadequacy of its military plans. From September, REVISE's commanders had relied upon the assurances of MI6 that a new Egyptian government was waiting to take power once British attacks had shaken Nasser's position. Eden had then combined REVISE with the façade of the ultimatum but neglected to tell his commanders of his true intentions. As a result, Britain was maintaining the pretence of keeping the peace between Egypt and Israel while tying to fight a war. Moreover, this was a war which did not rely upon the conventional strategy of superior force in the air and on the ground; instead, it relied upon bombing and psychological warfare to encourage the Egyptian people to strike the final blow against Nasser.

12.8 1956 3 September
Intelligence assessment of British military

NASSER'S position depends on a continuation of the present highly effective Police State controls and on his not having to suffer a public blow to his prestige. . . . The materialistically minded Egyptian civilian is unlikely long to sustain the rigours of wartime economy or the actual experience of battle and remain faithful to the Regime. It seems less likely to be a question of 'If there is a collapse of public morale and support for the Regime' as of how quickly that will take place.

Public Record Office, AIR20/9570, Doughty–Wylie report, 3 September 1956

Phase I of REVISE destroyed most of the Egyptian Air Force on 31 October, but there were ominous failures. The planes struggled with technical problems, and some bombers almost attacked American civilians being evacuated from Cairo. The US Sixth Fleet harassed the Anglo–French convoy carrying soldiers from Cyprus and Malta to Egypt, 'buzzing' it with aircraft and shadowing it with submarines. When surprised British commanders discovered that French and Israeli officers were conferring and French planes were attacking Egypt from bases inside Israel, they pressed Eden to cable French Prime Minister Guy Mollet, 'Nothing could do more harm to our role as peacemakers than to be identified in this way with one of the two parties.'[7] Most importantly, the military failed to keep the Suez Canal open. One Egyptian blockship was conveniently sunk by British bombers in the middle of the water way, and the Egyptians scuttled forty-eight more ships in following days.

All this was a roaring success, however, compared with the chaos that followed. Phase II relied upon psychological warfare 'to bring the Egyptians to the verge of surrender in a further six days', but the political limitations of 'peacekeeping' cancelled most of the operations.[8] Worried about civilian casualties, the Egypt Committee suspended the bombing of oil tanks, telephone and telegraph systems, and railway lines.

12.9   *1956   1 November*
Egypt Committee meeting

If Egyptian oil installations were attacked, other Arab countries might well retaliate against UK oil interests. . . . Moreover, apart from the odium we should incur as a result of any acts which resulted in widespread disease and suffering among the civilian population in Egypt, it was not in our long-term interests to cause serious damage to the Egyptian economy which we would subsequently need to repair during our occupation of parts of Egyptian territory.

Public Record Office, CAB134/1216, E.C.(56)37th meeting

The attack on Cairo Radio was delayed because the military thought the main transmitter was in the centre of Cairo; in fact, it was fifteen miles outside the city. The radio station was finally bombed on

[7] Public Record Office, PREM11/1132, Foreign Office to Paris, Cable 2863, 1 November 1956.
[8] Public Record Office, AIR8/2097, Allied Forces Headquarters to Air Ministry, Cable COSAIR/1, 1 November 1956.

2 November but was able to resume broadcasting within seventy-two hours.

The British plan to demoralise the Egyptian people with millions of leaflets dropped from airplanes was a fiasco. Canberra bombers were technically unable to carry out the drops, and Air Force Headquarters would not risk 'loosing valuable transport aircraft which were needed to mount the airborne assault'.[9] The fuses releasing the leaflets were often too powerful, leaving nothing more than fragments of paper for the Egyptian countryside. Eventually only one load of 500,000 leaflets was dropped, and two aircraft with loudspeakers were never used.[10]

The only part of Phase II that was fully implemented was broadcasting by radio stations, purportedly operated by Egyptian opponents of Nasser, into Egypt.

12.10 *1956 November*
Script for British 'black' radio station

Gamal Abdel Nasser promised a secure canal; he has brought war to the Canal. He promised the Egyptian people property and security; he has built a military machine at your expense and on your poverty; he promised the Egyptian people equality; he has given you dictatorship. He promised the Egyptian people peace; by provocation and defiance he has given you war.

Public Record Office, AIR20/10369, Memorandum for Director of Psychological Warfare, 3 November 1956

> Even this tactic soon failed, as the Arab staff of the BBC station in Cyprus, requisitioned for Government use, walked out. Some were later arrested for sabotaging the facilities and making pro-Egyptian broadcasts.
>
> In the end, Phase I never threatened Nasser's position.

12.11 *1956 November*
Statement of MI6 officer

Some young Egyptian officers, who were strongly opposed to Nasser, had been secured and . . . special weapons had been buried at a convenient spot near Cairo. They were never used

---

[9] Public Record Office, AIR8/2097, Third Summary of Operations, 2 November 1956.
[10] See Lucas (1991, pp. 272–3).

because certain circumstances essential to the operation did not materialise.

Chapman Pincher, *Inside Story*, London, 1978, p. 90

> When a former ally of Nasser asked him to surrender to the British Ambassador, the President refused. Instead he travelled in an open-top car through Cairo before cheering crowds, telling them, 'We shall fight to the last drop of our blood. We shall never surrender.'[11]
>
> It was now the Eden Government that was under pressure to give way. The top civil servant in the Foreign Office, Ivone Kirkpatrick, warned that Britain might have to leave the UN, and his junior officials in the Foreign Office considered mass resignation. The Attorney-General, Reginald Manningham-Buller, questioned the legality of the operation, and the Minister of Fuel and Power, Aubrey Jones, advised the Egypt Committee that oil consumption would have to be reduced by ten per cent to prepare for rationing. In the Commons, tension rose when Eden balked at the Labour Party's question if Britain was at war, and the sitting was suspended for the first time since 1924.[12]
>
> Most ominous was Macmillan's changing attitude. On the day of the Israeli attack, he told his Treasury officials that he would 'remain firm and see the affair through',[13] but he quickly retreated as British reserves of foreign currencies and gold dwindled. Those reserves were essential for Britain to buy necessary goods from overseas, such as machinery and agricultural products. Above all, with the Suez Canal blocked and a major oil pipeline across Syria blown up, Britain needed American dollars to pay for oil from the Western Hemisphere. Macmillan soon told his colleagues that the chance of success was only '51 to 49'.[14]

12.12   *1956   4 November*
Unnamed senior Cabinet Minister on Macmillan's message to Ministers

[He] could not be responsible for Her Majesty's Exchequer. . . . If sanctions were imposed on us, the country was finished.

Cited in Hugh Thomas, The Suez Affair, London, 1966, p. 146

[11] Cited in Heikal (1986, p. 196).
[12] See Lucas (1991, pp. 273–4).
[13] Public Record Office, T236/4188, Rowan memorandum, 31 October 1956.
[14] Cited in Clark (1986, p. 203).

Eden reacted to the growing crisis by inviting the United Nations to send a peacekeeping force to Egypt. He was gambling that it would take days, if not weeks, to organise the force and Britain and France could proceed in the interim. Once again, his mistake was to ignore the American reaction. By the time of a critical White House meeting on 1 November, the US had two more reasons to oppose the British venture. Firstly, the Eisenhower Administration was watching helplessly as Soviet tanks moved into Budapest to crush the Hungarian Revolution. While it is still unclear if the Soviets acted so aggressively because of the world's attention to Suez, the Americans argued that their hands were tied because of British and French behaviour in the Middle East. The Director of the CIA, Allen Dulles, asked his brother, Secretary of State Foster Dulles, 'How can anything be done about the Russians, even if they suppress the revolt, when our own allies are guilty of exactly similar acts of aggression?'[15] Secondly, OMEGA had collapsed. After months of planning, the CIA-backed coup in Syria, scheduled for 29 October, was foiled by the Israeli invasion of Egypt. Some American officials even suspected that the British had timed the Israeli attack to provoke disorder in Syria, allowing a takeover by Britain's ally Iraq. The Anglo-Iraqi plot was soon discovered by the Syrian authorities, who broke up the conspirators and sentenced thirteen to death.[16]

Despite their anger at the British, Eisenhower and his advisers still hoped to avoid a confrontation.

12.13 *1956 1 November*
Statement by President Eisenhower to the National Security Council

We must not permit ourselves to be blinded by the thought that *anything* we are going to do will result in our fighting with Great Britain and France. Such a course of action is simply unthinkable, and no one can possibly believe that we will do it.

Eisenhower Library, Eisenhower Papers, Ann Whitman Series, National Security Council, Box 8, 302nd NSC meeting

> The debate in the UN General Assembly, which included all members of the organisation, could not be avoided, however. Foster Dulles hoped to delay the session until 2 November, but UN rules required the debate to take place 24 hours earlier. The Secretary of State had no choice but to seize the initiative.

[15] Cited in Mosley (1978, p. 420).
[16] See Lucas (1991, pp. 276–7).

12.14   *1956   1 November*
Statement by Secretary of State Dulles to the National Security Council

For many years now, the US has been walking a tightrope between the effort to maintain our old and valued relations with our British and French allies on the one hand, and on the other try to assure ourselves fo the friendship and understanding of the newly independent countries who have escaped from colonialism. . . . Unless we now assert and maintain this leadership, all of these newly independent countries will turn from us to the USSR.

Eisenhower Library, Eisenhower Papers, Ann Whitman Series, National Security Council, Box 8, 302nd NSC meeting, 1 November 1956

> Foster Dulles' dilemma was evident in his speech to the General Assembly. He began, 'No delegate could have spoken with a heavier heart than I speak with tonight', for the US had to act against 'three nations with whom it has ties, deep friendship, admiration, and respect'. However, he could not accept the Anglo-French intervention: 'If, whenever a nation feels that it has been subjected to injustice, it should have the right to resort to force, . . . then I fear we should be tearing the Charter into shreds.' The General Assembly voted sixty-four to five for the American resolution for an immediate cease-fire.[17]
>
> Desperate, the French pressed the British for an immediate invasion of Egypt, with Israeli troops breaking the ultimatum and advancing to the east bank of the Suez Canal. After protracted debate, the British Cabinet rejected the proposal, but they agreed to consider an accelerated timetable for the landing at Port Said on the northern end of the canal.[18] This time, however, REVISE's commanders balked, fearing heavy Egyptian resistance with tanks.

12.15   *1956   2 November*
Cables from General Keightley, Commander-in-Chief of MUSKETEER REVISE, to British Chiefs of Staff

Any chances of an easy entry into Port Said are removed. As a result of today's photoreconnaissance, Egyptians are clearly

[17] Hoopes (1973, p. 379); Public Record Office, PREM11/1105, New York to Foreign Office, Cable 1009, 2 November 1956.
[18] Public Record Office, CAB134/1216, C.M.768(56), 2 November 1956.

going to resist our assault on Port Said with everything they have got.

Public Record Office, AIR8/1940, Cables KEYSEC 5 and KEYCOS 17

In the end, Keightley would only agree to an advance drop by para-troopers outside Port Said at dawn on 5 November.

The door had shut on British hopes. As late as 3 November, a high-ranking CIA official had held out hope of American acceptance of a British seizure of the Canal Zone.

12.16   *1956   3 November*
Telephone call by Robert Amory, CIA Deputy Director of Intelligence, to Chester Cooper, CIA representative in London

Tell your [British] friends to comply with the God-damn ceasefire or go ahead with the God-damn invasion. Either way, we'll back them up if they do it fast. What we can't stand is their God-damn hesita-tion, waltzing while Hungary is burning.

Chester Cooper, *The Lion's Last Roar*, London, 1978, p. 181

His words were eclipsed, however, when Foster Dulles was taken to hospital hours later with cancer of the colon. In the Secretary of State's absence, Secretary of the Treasury George Humphrey, who was unwill-ing to help Britain, was increasingly important because of his friend-ship with Eisenhower. State Department affairs were taken over by Acting Secretary of State Herbert Hoover, who had clashed with the British on Middle Eastern affairs in the past.

The collapse of Anglo-American co-operation was accompanied by public division within Britain. While the *Daily Express*, *Daily Mail*, and *Daily Telegraph* supported Eden, publications like *The Economist* turned against the war and *The Times* quoted Churchill to chastise the Government.

12.17   *1956   2 November*
Leader in *The Times*

I hold it perfectly justifiable to deceive the enemy, even if, at the same time, your own people are for a while misled. There is one thing, however, which all must never do, and that is mislead your ally.

'A lack of candour?', The Times, 2 November 1956, p. 9

A Gallup poll reported that only thirty-seven per cent of respondents thought Britain was 'right to take military action against Egypt' while forty-four per cent thought it was wrong.[19] The dissent peaked on the weekend of 3–4 November. In a rare Saturday sitting of the Commons, the Opposition shouted Lloyd down and Labour leader Gaitskell alleged, 'What [Britain] did was to go in and help the burglar and shoot the householder.' As Eden left the Chamber, the Labour front bench rose and called for his resignation.[20] The following day, more than 30,000 protestors gathered in Trafalgar Square to hear the prominent Labour politician Aneurin Bevan charge, 'Either Mr Eden is lying or he is too stupid to be Prime Minister.'[21]

Meanwhile, the situation at the United Nations went from catastrophe to catastrophe. Early on the morning of 4 November, the General Assembly adopted a second resolution, this one asking the UN Secretary-General to arrange a cease-fire within twelve hours. During the debate, the Israeli representative, Abba Eban, embarrassed the British by announcing that 'Israel agreed to a cease-fire, provided a similar announcement was forthcoming from Egypt'. This removed any excuse for British peacekeeping in the Suez Canal Base.[22]

On the afternoon of 4 November, the Cabinet gathered for a critical decision. The Egypt Committee had initially approved the paratroop drops for the next day but withdrew its decision in the face of Eban's announcement and threatened oil sanctions against Britain. Eden gave his Ministers three options: proceed with the occupation of Port Said, delay the airdrops for twenty-four hours, or defer action indefinitely. Twelve Ministers wanted to carry on, four voted for delay, and three favored an indefinite suspension.

12.18   *1956   4 November*
Cabinet meeting

The Prime Minister, summing up the discussion, said that it was evident that the overwhelming balance of opinion in the Cabinet was in favour of allowing the initial phase of the military operation to go forward as planned. This being so, he proposed that the United Nations should be informed that it remained necessary, in the view of the Governments of the United Kingdom and France, to interpose

---

[19] Public Record Office, PREM11/1123, Poole to Eden, 2 November 1956.
[20] See Jay (1980, p. 259).
[21] Avon Papers, AP20/30/1, Downing Street diary, 4 November 1956.
[22] Public Record Office, FO371/121747/VR1074/477, New York to Foreign Office, Cable 1047, 4 November 1956.

a force between Egypt and Israel in order to prevent the continuance of hostilities, to secure the speedy withdrawal of Israeli forces, to restore traffic through the Suez Canal and to promote a settlement of the outstanding problems of the area.

Public Record Office, CAB128/30, C.M.79(56)

> Despite the majority for action, the Prime Minister was shaken by the split in the vote and he temporarily adjourned the meeting to collect his thoughts. Only when he was told that the Israelis had retracted their agreement to a cease-fire did he regain his composure and press ahead.[23] He prepared Eisenhower with another futile plea:

12.19 *1956 5 November*
Letter from Prime Minister Eden to President Eisenhower

If we had allowed things to drift, everything would have gone from bad to worse. Nasser would have become a kind of Moslem Mussolini, and our friends in Iraq, Jordan, Saudi Arabia, and even Iran would gradually have been brought down. His efforts would have spread westwards, and Libya and North Africa would have been brought under his control.

Public Record Office, PREM11/1177, Foreign Office to Washington, Cable 5180, 5 November 1956

[23] See Rhodes James (1986, p. 566).

13

The downfall of Anthony Eden and the revival of the Anglo-American alliance

On 5 November, the UN General Assembly voted fifty-seven to none, with Britain, France, Israel, and sixteen other countries abstaining, for a cease-fire and a UN Emergency Force to be deployed in Egypt. As the vote was being taken, British and French paratroopers were occupying the main airfield and two bridges at the northern end of the Canal. Egyptian resistance was stiff, but Anglo-French casualties were minial and negotiations for the surrender of Port Said began at 5 p.m. The main Anglo–French landing by amphibious craft and helicopter followed at dawn the next day, and the force moved twenty-five miles down the Canal in the next eighteen hours.

By then, however, military success had been aborted by political failure. The Cabinet convened at 9:45 a.m. on 6 November. A handful of Ministers wanted to continue operations, but the opinion of the majority was decisive.

13.1   *1956   6 November*
Cabinet meeting

There was general agreement in the Cabinet that, in order to regain the initiative and to re-establish relations with those members of the United Nations who were fundamentally in sympathy with our aims, [Britain] should agree, subject to the concurrence of the French Government, to stop further military operations, provided that the Secretary-General of the United Nations could confirm that the Governments of Egypt and Israel had now accepted an unconditional cease-fire. . . .

Public Record Office, CAB128/30, C.M.80 (56)

French Prime Minister Mollet begged Eden for two more days to seize the rest of the canal Zone, but he could only get the agreement that the British would continue operations until midnight.[1]

The official reason for the British cease-fire was that peace had been obtained by the Anglo–French intervention, as Israel, after capturing its objectives in the Sinai Peninsula, had told the UN that it would stop fighting. The Cabinet's excuse was a charade, however, since the stated goal of restoring peace was always a mask for the seizure of the Canal and the overthrow of Nasser. Why then did Britain halt as its soldiers were advancing?

Three influences were significant. Firstly, the UN had cornered Britain. Eden had promised on 1 November that the British operations would be halted when the UN was ready to take over peacekeeping, and the General Assembly's authorisation of the UN Emergency Force on 5 November called his bluff. The British delegate, Pierson Dixon, told Eden that he 'thought that he could hold on at the UN until the end of the week',[2] but Lloyd and other Ministers cited UN opposition as a reason to cease fire.

13.2 *1956 6 November*
Statement by Foreign Secretary Lloyd to Cabinet

It was now urgently necessary that we should regain the initiative in bringing hostilities to an end while there was an opportunity to carry with us the more moderate sections of opinion in the General Assembly.

Public Record Office, CAB128/30, C.M.80(56)

Secondly, the Soviet Union had entered the picture with notes to Britain, France, and Israel carrying the none-too-subtle threat of military intervention.

13.3 *1956 5 November*
Soviet note to the Government of the United Kingdom

In what position would Britain have found herself if she herself had been attacked by more powerful states possessing every kind of modern destructive weapon? And there are countries now which

[1] See Love (1970, p. 626).
[2] Public Record Office, FO371/121748/VR1074/535, Foreign Office to New York, Cable 1565, 5 November 1956.

need not have sent a navy or air force to the coasts of Britain but could have used other means, such as rocket technique.

Middle East Affairs, January 1957, p. 11

It is doubtful that the British expected Soviet rocket attacks on London, but the prospect of Soviet troops or heavy equipment being transported into the Middle East was a frightening one.

Finally, the value of the pound was on the verge of collapse. In the first week of November, almost five per cent of Britain's reserves of foreign currencies and gold had been lost. At that rate, by early 1957 Britain would have no foreign currency to pay for essential imports. Chancellor of the Exchequer Macmillan was near panic when his American counterpart, George Humphrey, insisted 'that only a cease-fire by midnight would secure US support' of Britain's finances. He informed his colleagues that, without the cease-fire, he 'could not be responsible for Her Majesty's Exchequer'.[3]

The relative weight of these three influences is still debated by historians, though the most significant appears to be the threat of British economic collapse. Ultimately, however, it was the American position that linked all three factors, since US support would have delayed, if not prevented, UN resolutions, deterred the Soviets, and bolstered the pound. Eden admitted as much the day after the cease-fire.

13.4   *1956   7 November*
Memorandum by Prime Minister Eden

It is clear we cannot now carry this through alone with France. We must now get US support. . . . Our aim would be to get them to tackle an Anglo-US policy for a long-term settlement in the Middle East.

Public Record Office, PREM11/1105

Despite the catastrophic failures of the war, most British Ministers still thought the situation could be salvaged. The partial occupation of the Central Zone could be a lever in negotiations with Egypt. Anglo-French forces could not only occupy the Zone until UN troops arrive but remain as part of the UN Emergency Force. Meanwhile, Britain and France would maintain economic and financial pressure upon Egypt, and the OMEGA programme to overthrow Nasser could be renewed with American help.

[3] See Lloyd (1978, p. 209); Hugh Thomas (1966, p. 146).

13.5   1956   7 November
Ministerial agreement at Cabinet meeting

[Britain would] devote efforts to inducing [the Americans] to acknowledge the existence in the Middle East of the dangerous situation which they had consistently refused to recognise since the end of [World War II]. . . . [The Prime Minister] would endeavour to convince [the US] that a final decision by the UN on the composition and functions of the international force in the Suez Canal area should, if possible, be deferred until the Governments of the UK and the US had reached a clearer understanding on their common objectives in the Middle East.

Public Record Office, CAB128/30, C.M.81 (56)

Having received a friendly call from Eisenhower after the announcement of the cease-fire, Eden telephoned the President the next day to suggest an Anglo–American–French summit in Washington. Eisenhower was receptive since the dispute between Britain and the US was 'like a family spat',[4] but his advisers protested that any concession to Britain would jeopardise the American position in the UN and the Arab world. Initially, Eisenhower agreed to the summit with Eden, provided Britain made no challenge to the role of the UN Emergency Force, but Acting Secretary of State Hoover was not satisfied.[5] After another thirty minutes of discussion, Eisenhower called Eden to postpone the meeting, giving the weak excuse, 'I just don't see how we could do it now with so much on our plate.'

13.6   1956   7 November
Telephone call from President Eisenhower to Prime Minister Eden

I have just had a partial Cabinet meeting on this thing, & they think our timing is very, very bad, & I am calling to tell you about it. First, we have got to get quickly in some way a coordinated military intelligence view. . . .

Next, although I had a landslide victory last night, we are not like you, and we have lost both Houses of Congress. Therefore I have to have the Senate and house leaders in right now. . . .

[4] Eisenhower Library, Ann Whitman Series, Ann Whitman Diary Box 8, November 1956 Diary (2), Eden to Eisenhower and Eisenhower to Eden, 7 November 1956.
[5] See Lucas (1991, p. 299).

And then, finally, I find that the boys at the UN they are trying to put pressure on now are Egypt and Israel. They are trying to put the squeeze on them. The general opinion is that any meeting until that gets done would exacerbate the situation. . . . I am very anxious to talk to you and [French Prime Minister] Mollet about our future. But I do believe, in view of what my people say, we will have to postpone it a little bit. I am sorry.

Eisenhower Library, Eisenhower Papers, Ann Whitman Series, Ann Whitman Diary, Box 8, November 1956 Diary (2)

Privately, the President doubted the wisdom of cutting off the British.

13.7   1956   7 November
Statement from President Eisenhower to Sherman Adams, his Chief of Staff

Turning down Eden's request for a personal talk did not seem to him the right thing to do. . . . This was not the time to be so concerned about appearance and propriety.

Cited in Sherman Adams, First-Hand Report, London, 1962, p. 260

Unfortunately for the British, it was the State Department that was shaping American policy. After the exchanges with Eden, Eisenhower and Hoover visited Foster Dulles in hospital. The President put Eden's view that 'the Bear [the Soviet Union] is still the central enemy', but Foster Dulles backed Hoover's line that 'it was extremely important to get the British and French troops out of Egypt as soon as possible'. According to one observer, when Eisenhower persisted, the Secretary of State cut him off with a curt, 'I see!'[6]

Meeting the new British Ambassador, Harold Caccia, Eisenhower 'could not personally have been more friendly or indeed more forgiving',[7] but Britain's isolation was increasing. The UN General Assembly not only excluded British and French troops from the UN Emergency Force but demanded the withdrawal of Britain and France from Egypt 'in accordance with earlier resolutions'.[8] Led by Humphrey and

[6] Eisenhower Library, John Foster Dulles Papers, White House Memoranda, Chronological, Box 4, Meetings with the President, Macomber memorandum, 7 November 1956.
[7] Public Record Office, PREM11/1106, Washington to Foreign Office, Cable 2277, 9 November 1956.
[8] Public Record Office, CAB128/30, C.M.82(56), 8 November 1956.

Hoover, the Americans refused emergency oil shipments to Britain and blocked any financial relief for the pound.

13.8   *1956   8 November*
National Security Council meeting

Secretary Hoover commented that the Anglo-French cabal had not only 'kidded' the United States; it had also kidded the nations of the British Commonwealth and, to some extent, the British public too. ... The President agreed, and stated that this Government officially should keep out of the oil supply problem until we were assured that the cease-fire was in effect.

Eisenhower Library, Eisenhower Papers, Ann Whitman Series, National Security Council, Box 8, 303rd NSC meeting

To make matters worse, the Eden Government even had to contemplate facing Moscow alone as British military commanders worried about possible attacks by Soviet aircraft.

13.9   *1956   6 November*
Allied Forces Headquarters, Cyprus, to Air Ministry, London

Information has been received that Russia may intervene in the Middle East with force. Action will be taken forthwith so that all airfields are at the maximum state of preparedness for an attack against them.

Public Record Office, AIR8/1940, AFHQ to CINCMED and others, Cable CINC 145

Eden was now 'blacked out' by the Americans, except for an exchange of brief letters on 11 November with Eisenhower.[9] Instead, other British Ministers tried to repair the situation. When Lloyd was refused a meeting with Hoover, he used scare tactics reminiscent of MI6's plans.

---

[9] Public Record Office, PREM11/1177, Eden to Eisenhower and Eisenhower to Eden, 7 November 1956.

13.10   *1956   16 November*
Memorandum by President Eisenhower's Staff Secretary, Colonel Andrew Goodpaster

In a brief meeting which Mr. Hoover [Under-secretary of State], Admiral Radford [Chairman of the Joint Chiefs of Staff], Mr. Allen Dulles [Director of the CIA] and I attended with the President, Mr. Hoover reported that Lloyd had told Lodge [US Ambassador to the United Nations] of certain [British] operational intentions regarding Syria. The Iraqis and perhaps the Turks would be involved, and the partition of Jordan [between Iraq and Israel] seemed probable.

Eisenhower Library, Eisenhower Papers, Ann Whitman Series, DDE Diaries, Box 19, November 1956 Staff Memoranda, Goodpaster memorandum, 16 November 1956

> This was reinforced by the warnings of the British military of 'alleged overflying by Russian military aircraft, the Russian build-up in Syria, and the exposed position of Iran'.[10]
> Pressed by the CIA and the US military, Hoover finally met Lloyd, and French Foreign Minister Pineau told CIA Director Allen Dulles of France's own plans to replace the Syrian regime. The plans fell apart, however, as British and American spy planes found no Soviet presence in Syria and a 'rather depressed' Lloyd received no commitments from the Americans.[11] Instead, the hospitalised Foster Dulles allegedly rubbed the salt in Lloyd's wounds by asking, 'Selwyn, why did you stop [the attack against Egypt]?'[12]

13.11   *1956   17 November*
Foreign Secretary Lloyd cable to Foreign Office on meeting with Secretary of State Dulles

[Foster Dulles] had no complaint about our objective in our recent operations. In fact they were the same as those of the US, but he still did not think that our methods of achieving them were the right ones. Even so he deplored that we had not managed to bring down Nasser.

Avon Papers, AP20/25, Washington to Foreign Office, Cable 2307

[10] Eisenhower Library, Eisenhower Papers, White House Office, Office to the Staff Secretary, Subject, Alphabetical, Box 14, Intelligence Matters (2), Goodpaster memorandum, 15 November 1956.
[11] See Lucas (1991, pp. 305–7).
[12] See Lloyd (1978, p. 221).

The Chancellor of the Exchequer, Macmillan, and another senior Minister, Lord Privy Seal R. A. Butler, took over the initiative. Macmillan in particular needed Anglo-American co-operation. Not only was he responsible for the fragile British economy, but he was in a precarious personal position, having shifted from being the most vocal proponent of military action to the strongest advocate for a cease-fire.

Macmillan found his opening in the tenuous health of the Prime Minister. Even before Eden announced that he would be leaving for rest and recuperation in Jamaica, Macmillan was telling the US Ambassador, Winthrop Aldrich, that he could visit Washington as 'Eden's deputy', since 'Eden was very tired and should have a rest' before attending a summit. On 18 November, Macmillan went even further. He told Aldrich that Britain's foreign reserves would be exhausted within weeks and the country would shut down from lack of oil. However, there was going to be change, since the Cabinet was 'completely to be reshuffled and . . . Eden [was] going out because of sickness'.[13]

The effect on the Americans was immediate. Eisenhower, with the full support of Humphrey and Hoover, authorised further talks with Macmillan and Butler.

13.12   *1956   20 November*
Telephone call from President Eisenhower to Winthrop Aldrich, US Ambassador to Britain

EISENHOWER: You are dealing with at least one person – maybe two or three – on a very personal basis. Is it possible for you, without embarrassment, to get together the two that you mentioned in one of your messages.

ALDRICH: Yes. One of them I have just been playing bridge with. Perhaps I can stop him.

EISENHOWER: I'd rather you talk to both together. You know who I mean? One has same name as my predecessor at Columbia University [Butler]; the other was with me in the war [Macmillan].

Eisenhower Library, Eisenhower Papers, Ann Whitman Series, DDE Diaries, Box 19, November 1956 Telephone Calls

---

[13] US National Archives, Department of State, Central File, 974.7301/11 1956, London to State Department, Cable 2791, 19 November 1956.

When the State Department failed to block a General Assembly resolution calling for immediate withdrawal without conditions, Eisenhower finally circumvented those resisting reconciliation with the British. He told Hoover, 'We should give the British every chance to work their way back into a position of influence and respect in the Middle East.'[14] The Secretary of the Treasury, George Humphrey, assured Butler that, if Britain withdrew from Egypt, the US would not only supply loans and oil but also press the Egyptians to accept an international authority for the Suez Canal.[15]

Gradually, Butler and Macmillan led the Cabinet, unaware of the secret contacts with the Americans, to accept withdrawal from Egypt. The matter was sealed when Macmillan told Ministers that more than twenty per cent of Britain's reserves of foreign currency had been lost since September.[16] On 3 December, Lloyd told the House of Commons that British troops would withdraw by mid-December and that Britain would set no preconditions for negotiations on a Canal settlement.

13.13   1956   3 December
Statement by Foreign Secretary Lloyd to the House of Commons

The French and British Governments have come to the conclusion that the withdrawal of their forces in the Port Said area can now be carried out without delay. They have instructed the Allied Commander-in-Chief, General Keightley, to seek agreement with the UN Commander, General Burns, on a timetable for the complete withdrawal, taking account of the military and practical problems involved. This timetable will be reported as quickly as possible to the Secretary-General of the United Nations. Given good faith on all sides, it can be carried out in a short time.

Hansard, House of Commons, 3 December 1956, Vol. 561, Col. 882

Within three weeks, London received almost $2 billion in US-backed loans and aid.

Eden was unaware of the Butler–Macmillan discussions with the Eisenhower Administration. While in Jamaica, he tried to intervene against withdrawal but was told by Butler, 'Do not attempt to break your isolation.'[17]

---

[14] Eisenhower Library, Eisenhower Papers, Ann Whitman Series, DDE Diaries, Box 19, November 1956 Staff Memoranda, Goodpaster memorandum, 26 November 1956.
[15] Public Record Office, PREM11/1106, Humphrey to Butler, 26 November 1956.
[16] Public Record Office, CAB128/30, C.M.91(56), 29 November 1956.
[17] Cited in Rhodes James (1986, p. 587).

13.14 *1956 2 December*
Cable from Lord Privy Seal Butler to Prime Minister Eden

I know how difficult it must be for you to form a judgment without full knowledge of all that has gone on since you left. But we believe that the policy on which we have decided is consistent with the course which you set for us. We hope you will feel that we have taken the right decision.

Avon Papers, AP20/25, Colonial Office to Jamaica, Personal No. 20

> Thus, although he returned to Britain in mid-December to resume work, the Prime Minister had been eclipsed in all but name. Macmillan assured Foster Dulles that the transition was almost complete.

13.15 *1956 12 December*
Report by Secretary of State Dulles of conversation with Chancellor of the Exchequer Macmillan

[Macmillan] recognised that there had been a certain loss of confidence on the part of the President, myself, and others because of the Suez operation and the deception practiced upon us in that connection. . . . He, personally, was very unhappy with the way in which the matter was handled and the timing but . . . Eden had taken this entirely to himself and he, Macmillan, had had no real choice except to back Eden. . . .

After Eden returned, there would be a question as to whether he would resign at once on account of ill-health. If not, he would probably hold on for six months, but he would be a constitutional Prime Minister.

Eisenhower Library, John Foster Dulles Papers, General Correspondence and Memoranda, Box 1, L-M(2)

> When Eden entered the House of Commons on 17 December, there was almost complete silence, only a single Conservative MP rising to wave his order paper. Within days, he was resorting to outright deception of Parliament.

13.16   *1956   20 December*
Statement by Prime Minister Eden to the House of Commons

I want to say this on the question of foreknowledge and to say it quite bluntly to the House, that there was not foreknowledge that Israel would attack Egypt – there was not.

Hansard, House of Commons, 20 December 1956, Vol. 502, Col. 1457

Coincidentally, his recurrent ailments flared up, and he was told by his doctors that his health would be endangered if he stayed in office. On 9 January, Eden summoned his Cabinet and announced his resignation. A day later, Harold Macmillan, the man who had planned Eden's downfall, outmanoeuvred Butler to become Prime Minister.

14

Conclusion

On the surface, the impact of Suez quickly faded. Macmillan moved to repair the Anglo-American alliance, persuading Eisenhower and his advisers to accept summits at Bermuda in March 1957 and Washington in October. Britain remained in the Baghdad Pact and maintained its position in the oil-producing states of the Arabian Peninsula on the Persian Gulf. Significantly, Washington and London soon consulted about another *coup* in Syria. When American troops entered the Lebanon in June 1958 to keep a pro-Western Government in power, the Macmillan Government seized the opportunity to put paratroopers into Jordan in a show of unity.

Yet much of this was symbol rather than substance. Suez had exposed Britain's inability to act without the approval of the US; thus, any 'alliance' was controlled by Washington. The Eisenhower Doctrine of January 1957 established that the US, *alone* if necessary, would defend any Middle Eastern country against the Communist threat.

14.1 *1957 5 January*
Speech by President Eisenhower to the United States Congress

The United States, through the joint action of the President and the Congress, or, in the case of treaties, the Senate, has manifested in many endangered areas its purpose to support free and independent government – and peace – against external menace, notably the menace of International Communism. Thereby we have helped to maintain peace and security during a period of great danger. It is now essential that the United States should manifest, through joint action of the President and the Congress, our determination to assist those nations of the Middle East area which desire that assistance.

Documents on International Affairs, 1957, pp. 233–40

When Macmillan met the President in March, the Americans made it clear that Britain would have to accept a Suez Canal settlement and the loss of its influence in the Eastern Mediterranean.

Britain's decline in the Middle East was confirmed by the Iraqi Revolution of June 1958. King Feisal II and Britain's ally of more than forty years, Prime Minister Nuri Sa'id, were overthrown and killed, and the Baghdad Pact quickly disintegrated. The British paratroopers who entered Jordan left within weeks, leaving Macmillan to face reality. Britain, which had controlled most of the Middle East twenty years earlier, had been reduced to outposts in sheikhdoms like Abu Dhabi, Aden, and Kuwait.

It could be argued that this process was inevitable. By the 1950s, Britain did not have the resources to maintain its Empire. In many of its former colonies, nationalism was leading to demands for independence from Western influence. Militarily, the British could not compete with the emerging superpowers in the US and the USSR. So London steadily shed its commitments after World War II, beginning with withdrawal from India, Greece, and Palestine in 1947. Less than four years after Suez, Macmillan announced the final great retreat from Empire, announcing that the 'winds of change' sweeping Africa meant Britain would give up her colonial presence on that continent.

This does not mean, however, that Suez had no effect upon Britain's climbdown from global power. In the years before 1956, British officials had tried to replace 'colonialism' with 'partnership'. The strategy was not always effective, but in the Middle East, agreements like the 1954 Anglo-Egyptian Treaty and the Baghdad Pact held out the prospect of a continued British presence. This position would be assisted by a strong relationship with the Americans, whose military and economic resources could support Britain's diplomatic position.

Suez ruined these efforts. The collusion with Israel and France not only shattered British ties with Arab countries like Iraq and Jordan; it offered no benefits since the Israelis always saw Britain as a reluctant partner unworthy of trust and the French were angered by Eden's decision to cease fire while Allied forces were advancing. The damage to the Anglo-American relationship was partially repaired by Macmillan but a partnership of equals between Washington and London in the Middle East was now out of the question. Britain also lost the moral high ground before the United Nations and world opinion, with Suez compared to the crushing of the Hungarian Revolution by the Soviet Union.

So who was the villain of the drama? The question is somewhat misleading, for there were circumstances beyond any individual that contributed to the Suez Crisis. Eden operated within a British system in which groups like MI6 and Ministers like Macmillan were making their own plans, Nasser always had to consider his position with the Egyptian military, and Eisenhower was often less influential than Foster Dulles and Allen Dulles in the implementation of American policy. London, Washington, and Cairo were also affected by the actions of other countries, notably France, and regional considerations like the Arab-Israeli dispute, rivalry between Egypt and Iraq, and the pivotal position of Jordan. In short, Suez was not a simple conflict between Britain and Egypt or between East and West but a complex interaction between a number of political systems and an even larger number of policymakers.

Yet within that framework, Anthony Eden emerges as the pivotal figure, for it was his decisions that finally committed Britain to war and failure. Nasser's nationalisation of the Suez Canal may have been a challenge to the British position, but the Egyptian leader was not the menacing Mussolini or Hitler that Eden portrayed. Egypt's economic and military position was inferior to Israel, let alone the might of Western countries, and Egyptian 'expansion' consisted of a vague vision of Arab unity rather than conquest of neighbouring countries. Nor can Eden's other nemesis, Foster Dulles, take the blame for the war. It was probably unwise for the Secretary of State, trying to avoid a confrontation with the British, to keep devising new plans that held out the hope of Anglo-American action against Nasser over the nationalisation of the Canal. By mid-October, however, no one in the Eden Government could have misunderstood Washington's aversion to force.

Eden alone bears the responsibility for the decision of 14 October to collude with France and Israel. He may have been supported in this decision by Macmillan's desire for war, which led to assessments bordering on deception, and by the consent of other Ministers. He may have been guided towards his decision by the grandiose plans of his own intelligence service, MI6. He may have been pressed by French officials anxious to get rid of Nasser. However, the Prime Minister, having agreed to pursue a negotiated settlement of the Canal issued earlier on 14 October, could have refused the 'poisoned chalice' of co-operation with Israel.

Eden must also carry the burden of a second error. Having agreed to collusion, he insisted on the fiction of British 'peacekeeping' in the Middle East. A disguise which fooled no one, since it transparently helped the Israelis to take Egyptian territory, it also sabotaged the strategy of British military commanders. The psychological warfare of REVISE could only succeed in turning the Egyptian people against Nasser if British attacks destroyed civilian facilities, but Eden's charade prevented such an assault. Finally, under international pressure to keep his promise of 'peacekeeping', the Prime Minister had to cut short his last option, the occupation of the Canal Zone by British and French troops. The criticism of Eden's predecessor, Winston Churchill, was cutting and to the point: 'I am not sure I should have dared to start, but I am sure I should not have dared to stop.'[1]

This judgement of Eden may appear harsh. He had grown up in the heyday of the British Empire, become its chief diplomat in the 1930s, and helped it survive World War II. In 1995, living in a 'little Britain', the attempt at Suez to hold on to Britain's global position can easily be dismissed as foolhardy; forty years earlier, retreat from greatness was much harder to imagine. Yet Eden, as Foreign Secretary in the 1950s, had recognised the changing position of Britain.

14.2   1952   *June*
Memorandum by Foreign Secretary Eden

It is becoming clear that rigorous maintenance of the presently accepted policies of His Majesty's Government at home and abroad is placing a burden on the country's economy which is beyond the resources of the country to meet. . . . A choice of the utmost difficulty lies before the British people, for they must either give up, for a time, some of the advantages which a high standard of living confers upon them or, by relaxing their grip on the outside world, see their country sink to the level of a second-class power, with injury to their essential interests and way of life of which they can have little conception.

Public Record Office, CAB129 Series, C(52)202, 'Britain's Overseas Obligations'

During the course of the Suez Crisis, whether because of poor health, the pressure of the Premiership, rash temperament, or some other explanation, he lost this perspective on Britain's capabilities and limitations.

The history of Suez will never repeat itself. The Britain that existed before the event, both at home and abroad, was far different from that which was to follow. There is much to learn from the crisis, however. The complexity of Middle Eastern events is now part of everyday life; far less apparent but just as significant are the peculiarities of British

[1] Cited in Hugh Thomas (1966, p. 164).

policymaking and the fluid nature of the Anglo-American alliance. Most importantly, the story of Suez is one that establishes the irrational and unexplainable alongside the logical and practical in international politics.

Guide to further reading

General works: Britain

Given the importance of the Suez Crisis, both actual and symbolic, in Britain's decline as a Great Power after 1945, there are surprisingly few surveys of the event in English. The first, *The Secrets of Suez* was actually a short book by two French journalists, Merry and Serge Bromberger, which was quickly translated for British readers. Its chief value was to show how bitterly French politicians and military leaders felt about their 'betrayal' by their British colleagues, notably Prime Minister Anthony Eden's decision to cease fire before the Suez Canal Zone was occupied.

Several British books in the early 1960s, including Erskine Childers' *The Road to Suez*, A. J. Barker's *Suez: The Seven-Day War*, and Leon Epstein's *British Policy in the Suez Crisis*, gave straightforward accounts of the diplomatic and military aspects of the crisis; however, none explored 'hidden' aspects like collusion. The Canadian author Terence Robertson began to uncover some of the secret negotiations in his *Crisis: The Inside Story of the Suez Conspiracy*, but a comprehensive account only emerged in 1966 with Hugh Thomas's *The Suez Affair* and the BBC programme *Suez: Ten Years After*. Thomas's strength was his use of unnamed, often high-level, British and French sources; the BBC not only put some of those sources, notably French Foreign Minister Christian Pineau, on screen but also interviewed personalities like Nasser to give a rounded picture of the crisis.

Although there are minor errors in Thomas's account – for example, he placed the critical meeting between Eden and the

French envoys on 15 October, one day late – his overall depiction of the path to failure dominated British scholarship for more than twenty years. Few general books were published in the 1970s, and with British authors in the 1980s preferring the intricacies of Anthony Eden and Harold Macmillan (see section on memoirs and biographies below) to a full review of the crisis, even the opening of Government documents under the thirty-year rule had little immediate effect.

The first breakthrough came with an edited collection by W. R. Louis and Roger Owen, *Suez 1956: The Crisis and its Consequences*. The essays stemmed from conferences in London, Washington, and Tel Aviv in 1986–87, attended by both participants in the events of 1956 and academics researching them. The signficance of the collection lay in its diversity, with contributions from the US, Britain, France, Egypt, and Israel. Thus, while some of the essays were superficial at best, other contributions, notably those from Israeli authors Shimon Shamir and Michael Bar-On, broadened the perspective of Western readers.

This search for new interpretations combined with new materials culminated in two books in 1991, Keith Kyle's *Suez* and my *Divided We Stand: Britain, the US, and the Suez Crisis*. Beyond the publication date, there is little similarity between the two volumes. Kyle's distinction is his attempt for a comprehensive review of British material. Kyle tries to integrate his study of British foreign policy with an examination of issues like the Arab-Israeli dispute but, without a clear line of analysis, he falls back on traditional narrative, notably the portrait of Eden as a flawed but valiant leader. *Divided We Stand* is a slimmer work which, from the beginning, claims to put the Suez Crisis in a different perspective through the study of new influences, like the American and British intelligence services, and the effect of 'third' countries, notably France, the Arab States, and Israel. I believe the book is a necessary revision to the standard British-centred accounts of Suez, but sometimes it may be too ambitious, notably in its speculation of a Franco-Israeli 'conspiracy' to draw Britain into the attack upon Egypt and its castigation of both Eden, for hasty and ill-judged decisions, and Macmillan, for deviousness. The paperback version of this book, to be published in 1996, reconsiders these interpretations.

General works: other countries

The Suez Crisis had far less of an effect upon the United States, established as a superpower by 1956 and soon preoccupied with other Cold War matters; accordingly, there are few histories by American authors. The first, Herman Finer's *Dulles Over Suez*, was a sustained attack upon John Foster Dulles and, to a lesser degree, Gamal Abdel Nasser rather than a balanced analysis of events. Fortunately, this was followed by Kennett Love's masterful, if lengthy, approach in *Suez: The Twice-Fought War*. Love placed his study of American and British policies and personalities within the Byzantine politics of the Middle East, examining the effects of Arab–Israeli tension and inter-Arab politics upon the development of the crisis. Often overlooked because of its emphasis upon analysis rather than revelation, Love's work is still effective after twenty-five years.

There matters stood until the debate in the 1980s over the nature of President Eisenhower's leadership (see section on memoirs and biographies below) brought a reconsideration of Suez. The 'revisionist' portrait of Eisenhower, rather than Foster Dulles, directing policy was evident in Donald Neff's *Warriors at Suez*. Neff's book was also the first to incorporate declassified American documents, although its effectiveness was limited by its narrow focus upon US foreign policy.

Two recent books have gone even further than Neff, trying to set Suez in a regional or Anglo-American context. Peter Hahn's *The US, Great Britain and Egypt, 1945–1956* is a valuable contribution, tracing the emerging importance of Egypt in American foreign policy in the 1950s. Hahn avoids black-and-white conclusions about 'alliance' and judgements about the key actors to portray the complexity of the background to Suez. In contrast, Stephen Freiberger's *Dawn over Suez* is limited by its assumption of conflict between Britain and the United States, which soon turns to a clichéd portrayal of relations between London and Washington, and a shortage of new evidence.

Despite the steady stream of memoirs by French participants in Suez, there is still no effective account of the crisis by a French historian. The greatest obstacle is the limited declassification of documents by the French Government; the material released has come from ministries which had a small role in the crisis, while the documents of the 'inner circle' of Ministers and military leaders involved in the collusion with Britain and Israel are still withheld from public view. Thus, the one contribution in English, Maurice Vaisse's article in the Louis/Owen collection (cited above), is limited to an assessment of the attitude of the French Foreign Office.

As in France, the opening of archives in Israel has been restricted with access to some material, especially military records, only granted to selected researchers. Israeli historians have made good use of memoirs, interviews, and the documents that have been opened, however, with valuable publications available in English and French. Michael Bar-Zohar's *Suez Ultra-Secret* (1964) developed the story of the Franco-Israeli alliance and his biographies of Prime Minister David Ben-Gurion added further information. More recently, Selwyn Ilan Troen and Moshe Shemesh's edited collection, *The Suez-Sinai Crisis of 1956: Retrospective and Reappraisal*, has several incisive essays and extracts from Ben-Gurion's diary. Michael Bar-On, who was Ben-Gurion's private secretary at the Sèvres meetings in 1956, is expected to develop his essay in Louis/Owen (cited above) into a book which should add both to the stock of primary evidence and interpretation of Israel's relations with Arab States and with Western powers. Meanwhile, Avi Shlaim's article, 'Conflicting Approaches to Israel's Relations with the Arabs: Ben-Gurion and Sharett, 1953–6' in the *Middle East Journal* is an outstanding and provocative work on the tensions within Israeli policymaking, and Michael Oren's reconsideration of Shlaim in 'Secret Egyptian–Israeli Peace Initiatives Prior to the Suez Campaign' in the *Middle East Journal* is also valuable.

With archives almost non-existent in Arab countries, there has been little of note published in English. Mohammed Heikal, a self-described adviser to President Nasser in the 1950s, has published two controversial books, *Nasser: The Cairo Documents* and *Cutting the Lion's Tail*. Both profess to have Heikal's first-hand accounts of the events before and during Suez; unfortunately, the documents in the Arabic editions of the books have not been translated. Many authors are sceptical of Heikal's claims, given his tendency for exaggeration and concern for his reputation, but as some of his material has been corroborated by other sources in Britain and the US, the books are of use to the careful reader. The only significant historical study is Mohammed Sayed-Ahmed's *Nasser and American Foreign Policy, 1952–1956*, which is drawn primarily from British and American archival material supplemented by the author's knowledge of modern Egypt.

Specialist works

With many of the general studies of Suez centring upon the diplomatic process of 1956, any review of the crisis should take in books and articles focusing upon other aspects of the conflict.

For the background on British policy in the Middle East, the dominant work continues to be William Roger Louis's *The British Empire in the Middle East, 1945–51*. The 803-page book sometimes sacrifices analysis for detail and it is frustratingly vague on the nature of the Anglo–American relationship in the Middle East, but it is still essential reading. With the emergence of new material, previous work on the British position in the region is increasingly out-of-date, although Elizabeth Monroe's *Britain's Moment in the Middle East, 1914–71* still works as an overview.

There is a curious lack of literature on Britain, the US, and the Middle East in the 1950s. Until an enterprising historian fills the gap, a reader has to draw the picture from scattered studies. Notable among these are David Devereaux's *The Formulation of British Defence Policy Towards the Middle East*, which is particularly strong on military strategy; Geoffrey Aronson's *From Sideshow to Centre Stage: US Policy Towards Egypt, 1946–56*; Ayesha Jalal's 'Towards the Baghdad Pact: South Asia and Middle Eastern Defence in the Cold War, 1947–55' in the *International History Review*; and W. S. Lucas's 'The Path to Suez: Britain and the Struggle for the Middle East, 1953–6' in Anne Deighton (ed.), *Britain and the First Cold War*.

The best overview of the military dimension of Suez is still Roy Fullick and Geoffrey Powell's *Suez: The Double War* although recent articles are beginning to develop new information on national strategies. Anthony Gorst and W. S. Lucas try to integrate British political and military strategy in 'Suez 1956: Strategy and the Diplomatic Process' in the *Journal of Strategic Studies*. Israeli preparations have been examined effectively by Raymond Cohen in 'Israeli Military Intelligence before the 1956 Sinai Campaign' in *Intelligence and National Security* and by Yigal Sheffy in 'Unconcern at Dawn, Surprise at Sunset: Egyptian Intelligence Appreciations before the Sinai Campaign, 1956' in *Intelligence and National Security*.

The economic dimension of Suez, essential to the understanding both of Britain's decision to attack Egypt and then to cease fire, was long overlooked, except for Jacob Abadi's *Britain's Withdrawal from the Middle East, 1947–71: The Economic and Strategic Imperatives*. Diane Kunz's *The Economic Diplomacy of the Suez Crisis* is considered by many to be the 'breakthrough' work on the topic, although it is weakened by Kunz's portrayal of economics as the dominant aspect of Suez, an approach that unnecessarily shoves aside all other considerations. Although it has received less attention, Lewis Johnman's 'Defending the Pound: The Economics of the Suez Crisis, 1956' in Anthony Gorst *et al.* (eds.), *Post-War Britain: Themes and Perspectives, 1945–64* is more effective in integrating economics with diplomacy, military strategy, and the role of personality.

The area of Suez most in need of exploration continues to be the role of the intelligence services, notably the British plans to assassinate or overthrow Nasser. Anthony Verrier's *Through the Looking Glass: British Foreign Policy in an Age of Illusions*, Nigel West's *The Friends: Britain's Post-War Secret Intelligence Operations*, and, most famously, Peter Wright's *Spycatcher* all claim to provide inside information but are damaged by a lack of reliability. The accuracy of Miles Copeland's *The Game of Nations* on American plans is also debated, although most of Copeland's claims have been sustained by other evidence. An overlooked jewel is *The Eden Legacy* by Geoffrey MacDermott, who was the operational liaison between the Foreign Office and MI6 in 1956. Although MacDermott was increasingly cut off from information as the crisis progressed, his first-hand account of British intrigues against Egypt is still unmatched.

The opportunity for historians to enter the field has been indicated by two articles on American and British plans to overthrow the Syrian Government, Douglas Little's 'Cold War and Covert Action: The United States and Syria, 1945–58' in the *Middle East Journal* and Anthony Gorst and W. S. Lucas's 'The Other Collusion: Operation Straggle and Anglo-American Intervention in Syria, 1955–6' in *Intelligence and National Security*. Richard Aldrich's 'Intelligence, Anglo-American Relations, and the Suez Crisis' is a useful review in the same journal.

The role of 'information services', notably those in Britain, also needs examination. The controversy over the BBC's domestic presentation of the Suez Crisis, which angered Prime Minister Eden and nearly produced formal Government machinery to control the BBC's output, has been covered in most general works and considered at length in Asa Briggs's *The BBC: The First Fifty Years*. However, the BBC was also involved in a comprehensive British campaign to overthrow Nasser through psychological warfare. The campaign included newspapers and radio stations which were secretly funded by the British Government, 'black' operations run by MI6, and the leaflet drops and loudspeaker programmes of the British military. Apart from limited consideration of the topic in Peter Partner's *Arab Voices: The BBC Arabic Service, 1938–88*, the field is wide open.

Memoirs and biographies: Britain

In contrast to the shortage of 'academic' work on some areas of Suez, there is an over-abundance of personal accounts and biographies concerned with the crisis. Many of those involved in the events of 1956, especially on the British side, were concerned to clear themselves of any blame; ironically, their contributions only fuelled controversy.

On the British side, the trail began with Anthony Eden, who began the attempt to protect his reputation soon after he left 10 Downing Street. His desire was only accentuated by the rapid publication of the Brombergers' book (cited above), a vehicle for attacks upon Eden by French leaders, and he also had to contend with *Anthony Eden*, a 'biography' by Randolph Churchill, the nephew of the former Prime Minister, notable only for the hatred displayed towards Eden.

Eden's response came in *Full Circle*. Because of the concern with clearing his name, the memoir is revealing, both about Eden's feelings and the development of British policy, even as it obscures, ignores, or lies about events such as the British collusion with France and Israel. *Full Circle* is still essential, provided the reader recognises its bias and checks its information against other sources.

Other Ministers in the Eden Government soon followed into print, with varying degrees of critical and commercial success. The Lord Chancellor, Lord Kilmuir, wrote *Political Adventure*, of which little is memorable. The recollections of the Lord Privy Seal, 'Rab' Butler, *The Art of the Possible*, are more forthcoming, although

Butler's portrayal of his troubled conscience over Suez does not exactly match the evidence of 1956. Meanwhile, Harold Macmillan, the man who succeeded Eden, published *Riding the Storm, 1956–9*. On the surface, the book includes a full survey of Suez, but its prose, contrasted with the personality of the writer, is flat and leaves the impression that Macmillan does not reveal all. Foreign Secretary Selwyn Lloyd's recollections in *Suez 1956* are overshadowed by his extraordinary attempt to explain how the British meetings with the French and Israelis at Sèvres did not constitute collusion.

Arguably, the most revealing insights into Suez and the men behind it come from authors who were outside the Cabinet but had close connections to Eden and other Ministers. The abridged diaries of Evelyn Shuckburgh, Assistant Secretary of State in the Foreign Office, *Descent to Suez* are always entertaining and informative, particularly about Eden in public and private. Shuckburgh's contribution ends in early 1956, but the diaries of William Clark, Eden's Press Secretary, *From Three Worlds* pick up the story vividly, tracing the problems both within the British Government and between Britain and 'allies' like the US. There is also the strange tale of Robert Henriques, the Anglo–Jewish farmer and World War II veteran who embarked on a private mission for Anglo–Israeli co-operation, in two articles in the *Spectator* in 1959.

Yet it is Anthony Nutting's *No End of A Lesson*, the memoir that fully revealed British collusion with France and Israel, that remains most provocative. Nutting's account is coloured by his rift with Eden, and Nutting, while playing up his resignation as Minister of State at the Foreign Office during the Suez War, plays down his public support, which is evident as late as mid-October 1956, for a strong stand against Eden. Still, this is a vivid memoir which contains information which is still withheld by the British Government.

Taken together, the memoirs shaped a debate which has continued in biographical accounts. Sidney Aster's *Anthony Eden* was a brief but uninspiring contribution; the battle was really joined between David Carlton with *Anthony Eden* and Robert Rhodes James with *Anthony Eden*. Carlton's account is a sustained attack upon Eden's entire career from his rise in the 1930s to his downfall at Suez. Although the book is sometimes hindered by Carlton's animosity, the range of sources still makes this the best account of Eden during the Suez Crisis, portraying a Prime Minister who was constantly on and sometimes over the edge of rational behaviour. In contrast, Rhodes James's biography, while admitting the shortcomings of Eden's actions during the crisis, is careful to portray any failure as the lapse of a well-intentioned and courageous politician. The result is a sustained apology which cannot account for the complexity of events that led to British collusion with France and Israel.

There have been two other studies of Eden in the last decade. Richard Lamb's *The Failure of the Eden Government* has some valuable information from Government documents, especially when compared with Rhodes James' use of Eden's own notes and diaries, but is marred by glaring errors of fact and analysis. Victor Rothwell's *Anthony Eden* contains little that is new or illuminating.

Beyond Eden, the figure who deserves the most attention is Macmillan. He was not only the Minister who profited from Suez, taking over at 10 Downing Street, but also the one figure who dramatically reversed course, insisting upon a British showdown with Nasser only to call for a cease-fire soon after military operations began. Yet it has been difficult to overcome Macmillan's own attempt to define his place in history through his six volumes of memoirs and his interviews with other authors.

For years, historians avoided a review of Macmillan, with Anthony Sampson's *Macmillan: A Study in Ambiguity* offering no more than a surface portrayal of Macmillan. The 'definitive' account finally came in 1988 with the first volume of Alistair Horne's *Macmillan*, which took ten years of research, but the results have been counter-productive. Horne's book is a vivid portrayal of the man but it is a portrayal based primarily on Macmillan's papers, notably his diary, and oral recollections. The result is a whitewash of Macmillan's role in Suez, portraying him as a marginal player in the final decision to attack Egypt. Several authors are working on more balanced interpretations of Macmillan, but until their publication, the reader has to rely on accounts in general works and, ironically, David Carlton's description of Macmillan within his biography of Eden (cited above).

Other useful memoirs and biographies of British participants in Suez include the first-hand account of Humphrey Trevelyan, the British Ambassador to Egypt, in *The Middle East in Revolution*, Anthony Howard's portrayal of R. A. Butler in *Rab*, D. R. Thorpe's *Selwyn Lloyd*, and *The Diary of Hugh Gaitskell, 1945–56*, edited by Philip Williams. The diaries of Pierson Dixon, the British

Ambassador to the United Nations, have been edited by Piers Dixon in *Double Diploma* but contribute little on Suez.

Memoirs and biographies: other countries

Although Suez is far from a dominant event in American history, the controversy over the reputation of John Foster Dulles and, later, the effectiveness of President Dwight Eisenhower has produced a wealth of material on US policymakers in the crisis. Interestingly, it was Anthony Eden's memoirs (cited above) that started the debate. Eisenhower was upset at what he believed was an inaccurate account of Suez which unfairly criticised his Administration, particularly Secretary of State Dulles. Since Foster Dulles had died in 1959, Eisenhower made a lengthy defence in his own memoirs, *The White House Years: Mandate for Change, 1953–1956* and *The White House Years: Waging Peace, 1956–1961*. Eisenhower's reply is revealing about his own perceptions of the crisis, but it suffers from blandness of expression and the calculated attempt to project himself as peacemaker. Thus, the reader would search in vain for any reference to OMEGA, the Anglo-American plan to overthrow Nasser, or for the American collaboration with British Ministers to ease Eden from power after Suez.

With Foster Dulles leaving no account of Suez and other key officials, notably Secretary of the Treasury George Humphrey and CIA Director Allen Dulles, also declining to write memoirs, the other significant autobiographies come from four men who were outside the Cabinet but well-placed to observe American policy. Robert Murphy, the third-highest official in the State Department and a key figure in the early stages of the Suez Crisis, left a vivid depiction in *Diplomat Among Warriors*. The book is bitter about British actions during Suez but makes no effort to distort the record in Murphy's favour. Similarly, Chester Cooper, the CIA liaison in London in 1956, gives an account in *The Lion's Last Roar* which reveals how US officials were torn between support and hostility for their British ally. Sherman Adams, Eisenhower's Chief of Staff, touched on Suez in *First-Hand Report* to no great effect, but Emmet Hughes, one of Eisenhower's speechwriters, stirred controversy with *The Ordeal of Power: The Inside Story of the Eisenhower Administration*, which claimed animosity between Eisenhower and Foster Dulles and portrayed the Secretary of State as a bumbling ideologue.

Herman Finer's near-hysterical assault upon Foster Dulles in *Dulles Over Suez* (cited above) fuelled the debate over the Secretary of State's effectiveness. Other accounts, notably J. R. Beal's *John Foster Dulles*, Roscoe Drummond and Gaston Coblenz's *Duel at the Brink*, and Louis Gerson's *John Foster Dulles* were kinder without adding much information. Instead, it was Townsend Hoopes who offered an entertaining, well-researched, and complex portrait in *The Devil and John Foster Dulles*, which shows the intensity of Foster Dulles' beliefs while recognising his strengths and weaknesses. Leonard Mosley's *Dulles*, a double biography of Foster Dulles and Allen Dulles, should be read for its anecdotes, but its evidence is very suspect and should not be accepted without corroboration.

Whatever their opinion of Foster Dulles, all these biographies had assumed that the Secretary of State, rather than the President, was the key man behind US foreign policy. Until recently, accounts of Eisenhower agreed. Marquis Childs's *Eisenhower: Captive Hero* is well-written if out-of-date while Peter Lyon's *Eisenhower: Portrait of a Hero* is informative but uninspiring and very long. Herbert Parmet's *Eisenhower and the American Crusade*, Robert Divine's *Eisenhower and the Cold War*, and William Ewald's *Eisenhower the President* neatly package the standard evidence without great insight.

The 'breakthrough' work on Eisenhower was Stephen Ambrose's *Eisenhower the President*, a skilful portrait which recasts the President as an expert policymaker, delegating the implementation to his officials while developing the principles and guidelines. In Suez, for example, Eisenhower is no longer the spectator of Foster Dulles' diplomatic manipulations but the President who defines the American mission to hold on to its alliances while preventing war. In combination with more limited studies, notably Fred Greenstein's *The Hidden-Hand Presidency* and Stephen Ambrose and Richard Immerman's *Ike's Spies*, the book's argument was compelling.

Unfortunately, Ambrose went too far. While Eisenhower was the controlling influence in some cases, his knowledge of certain areas of the world and, thus, his effectiveness in policymaking were woefully inadequate. This was especially true of the Middle East. So Eisenhower, up to July 1956, allowed Foster Dulles to make the key decisions, and during the Suez War, the President's indecisiveness first produced ambiguity and then, after Foster Dulles' hospitalisation, a policy hostile to the British. The latest studies of Eisenhower and his officials, particularly Richard Immerman's edited collection, *John Foster Dulles and the Diplomacy of the Cold War*, have followed Ambrose's line without addressing its shortcomings. Until the pendulum swings to a more balanced view, the reader should consider Blanche Cook's *The Declassified Eisenhower*, a little-known work which is full of revelations and insight into the complexities of the Eisenhower Administration.

The recollections of French leaders on the crisis are dominated by Foreign Minister Christian Pineau's account in *Suez 1956*. Pineau had already made his opinions clear to several authors, and his colourful memoirs package his disdain for Nasser and the Eden Government which abandoned the Suez operation. The book freely admits the secret French relationship with Israel but never stops to consider that policy might have been misguided. This should be read as a polemic rather than a balanced account.

Apart from Pineau, the French contributions come from the military and officials in the Ministry of Defence. General Maurice Challe, intimately involved with the collusion against Egypt, devoted a section of *Notre Révolte* to Suez, and General André Beaufre, the commander of French land forces, contributed *The Suez Expedition*. Like Pineau's work, the books only reaffirm what has already been told to others, serving more as non-stop criticisms of France's betrayal by all except Israel, but their vehemence makes them interesting reading. The account of Abel Thomas, who served at the Ministry of Defence in 1956, in *Comment Israël fut sauvé* is not as emotional but its careful recitation of events makes it essential for those who read French. In contrast, General Jacques Baeyens's *Un Coup d'épée dans l'eau du canal* is a slim effort, and Jacques Massu's *Vérité sur Suez* only adds a bit of detail. Surprisingly, given the interesting character of the Socialist-led Government of Guy Mollet and its involvement in Suez and Algeria, there are no significant biographies in English of the leading members.

The richness of Israeli memoirs and biographies is partial compensation for the restriction on that country's archives. Prime Minister David Ben-Gurion did not write an account, preferring to leave his papers and memories to biographers, but his top military commander, General Moshe Dayan, the Israeli Chief of Staff, offered a great deal of information in *Diary of the Sinai Campaign* and added to the tale in *The Story of My Life*. The controversial

Ariel Sharon, who led the initial paratroop drop into Egypt and barely avoided disaster, gives a brief but interesting description in *Warrior: An Autobiography*. Foreign Minister Golda Meir's *My Life* is disappointing, but the Israeli Ambassador to the United States, Abba Eban, offers an interesting perspective in *An Autobiography*. Gideon Raphael, an official in the Israeli Foreign Ministry who handled secret negotiations with Egypt before Suez, offers useful background in *Destination Peace: Three Decades of Israeli Foreign Policy*.

The quality of Michael Bar-Zohar's work on Ben-Gurion (cited above) has not been matched, but Matti Golan's *Shimon Peres*, the story of the future Prime Minister who was in the Ministry of Defence in 1956, adds colour to the tale of Franco-Israeli co-operation.

Contributions in English from the Arab world are almost nonexistent. President Gamal Abdel Nasser left no memoirs before his sudden death in 1970, and the recollections of his former adviser, Mohammed Heikal, (cited above) are often suspect. Jean Lacouture's *Nasser* has little to offer. Anthony Nutting followed his memoirs with *Nasser*, which is an interesting corrective to the portrait of Nasser as anti-British villain but has little new material.

Two other memoirs from key participants deserve a look. Robert Menzies, the Australian Prime Minister who led the mission in September 1956 that failed to get Nasser's acceptance of international control of the Suez Canal, has left a vivid account in *Afternoon Light*; unfortunately, his disdain for Nasser yields bias to the point of inaccuracy. In *Memoirs, Volume II, 1948–57: The International Years*, Canadian Foreign Minister Lester Pearson, who led the efforts at the United Nations to obtain a cease-fire, offers sober but revealing testimony about events before and during the Suez War.

Bibliography

Abadi, Jacob (1971), *Britain's Withdrawal from the Middle East, 1947–71: The Economic and Strategic Imperatives*, London

Adams, Sherman (1962), *First-Hand Report*, London

Aldrich, Richard (1994), 'Intelligence, Anglo-American Relations, and the Suez Crisis', *Intelligence and National Security* (July 1994)

Ambrose, Stephen (1982), *Eisenhower the President*, London

Ambrose, Stephen and Immerman, Richard (1981), *Ike's Spies*, New York

Aronson, Geoffrey (1986), *From Sideshow to Centre Stage: US Policy Towards Egypt, 1946–56*, Boulder, Colorado

Aster, Sidney (1976), *Anthony Eden*, London

Baeyens, Jacques (1976), *Un Coup d'épée dans l'eau du canal*, Paris

Bar-Zohar, Michael (1964) *Suez Ultra-Secret*, Paris

Bar-Zohar, Michael (1967), *The Armed Prophet: A Biography of Ben-Gurion*, London

Barker, A. J. (1964), *Suez: The Seven-Day War*, London

Beal, J. R. (1959), *John Foster Dulles*, New York

Beaufre, André (1969), *The Suez Expedition* London

Brands, H. W. (1989), 'The Cairo–Tehran Connection in Anglo-American Rivalry in the Middle East', *International History Review* (August 1989)

Briggs, Asa (1985), *The BBC: The First Fifty Years*, Oxford

Bromberger, Merry and Bromberger, Serge (1957) (translated by James Cameron), *The Secrets of Suez*, London

Butler, R. A. (1971), *The Art of the Possible*, London

Calvocoressi, Peter (1967), *Suez: Ten Years On*, London

Carlton, David (1981), *Anthony Eden*, London

Challe, Maurice (1968), *Notre Révolte*, Paris

Childers, Erskine (1962), *The Road to Suez*, London

Childs, Marquis (1959), *Eisenhower: Captive Hero*, London

Churchill, Randolph (1958), *Anthony Eden*, London

Clark, William (1986), *From Three Worlds*, London

Bibliography

Cohen, Raymond (1988), 'Israeli Military Intelligence before the 1956 Sinai Campaign', *Intelligence and National Security* (January 1988)

Cook, Blanche (1981), *The Declassified Eisenhower*, Garden City, New York

Cooper, Chester (1978), *The Lion's Last Roar*, London

Copeland, Miles (1969), *The Game of Nations*, London

Cosgrave, Patrick (1981), *R. A. Butler*, London

Dayan, Moshe (1967), *Diary of the Sinai Campaign*, London

Dayan, Moshe (1976), *The Story of My Life*, London

Deighton, Anne (ed.) (1990), *Britain and the First Cold War*, London

Devereaux, David (1990), *The Formulation of British Defence Policy Towards the Middle East*, Basingstoke

Divine, Robert (1981), *Eisenhower and the Cold War*, Oxford

Dixon, Piers (ed.) (1968), *Double Diploma*, London

Drummond, Roscoe and Coblenz, Gaston (1961), *Duel at the Brink*, London

Eban, Abba (1977), *An Autobiography*, New York

Eden, Anthony (1960), *Full Circle*, London

Eisenhower, Dwight (1963), *The White House Years: Mandate for Change, 1953–6*, London

Eisenhower, Dwight (1966), *The White House Years: Waging Peace, 1956–61*, London

Epstein, Leon (1964), *British Policy in the Suez Crisis*, London

Eveland, Wilbur (1980), *Ropes of Sand*, London

Ewald, William (1981), *Eisenhower the President*, Englewood Cliffs, New Jersey

Finer, Herman (1964), *Dulles Over Suez*, London

Freiberger, Stephen (1992), *Dawn Over Suez*, Chicago

Fullick, Roy, and Powell, Geoffrey (1979), *Suez: The Double War*, London

Gerson, Louis (1967), *John Foster Dulles*, New York

Gilbert, Martin (1988), *Winston S. Churchill, Volume VIII: Never Despair, 1945–1965*, London

Golan, Matti (1982), *Shimon Peres*, London

Gorst, Anthony, Lewis Johnson and W. Scott Lucas (eds) (1989) *Post-War Britain: Themes and Perspectives, 1945–64*, London

Gorst, Anthony and Lucas, W. Scott (1988a), 'The Other Collusion: Operation Straggle and Anglo-American Intervention in Syria, 1955–6', *Intelligence and National Security* (July 1988)

Gorst, Anthony and Lucas, W. Scott (1988b), 'Suez 1956: Strategy and the Diplomatic Process', *Journal of Strategic Studies* (December 1988)

Greenstein, Fred (1982), *The Hidden-Hand Presidency*, New York

Hahn, Peter (1991), *The US, Great Britain, and Egypt, 1945–1956*, Chapel Hill, North Carolina

Heikal, Mohammed (1972), *Nasser: The Cairo Documents*, London

Heikal, Mohammed (1986), *Cutting the Lion's Tail*, London

Henriques, Robert (1959a), 'The Ultimatum: A Dissenting View', *Spectator*, 6 November 1959

Henriques, Robert (1959b), 'The Ultimatum', *Spectator*, 4 December 1959

Hoopes, Townsend (1973), *The Devil and John Foster Dulles*, Boston

Horne, Alistair (1988), *Harold Macmillan: Volume I, 1894–1956*, London

Howard, Anthony (1987), *Rab*, London

Hughes, Emmet (1963), *The Ordeal of Power: The Inside Story of the Eisenhower Administration*, London

Immerman, Richard (ed.) (1989), *John Foster Dulles and the Diplomacy of the Cold War*, Princeton, New Jersey

Jalal, Ayesha (1989), 'Towards the Baghdad Pact: South Asia and Middle Eastern Defence in the Cold War, 1947–55', *International History Review* (August 1989)

Jay, Douglas (1980), *Change and Fortune*, London

Johnman, Lewis (1989), 'Defending the Pound: The Economics of the Suez Crisis, 1956', in Anthony Gorst, Lewis Johnman, and W. Scott Lucas (eds), *Post-War Britain: Themes and Perspectives, 1945–64*, London

Kilmuir, Lord (1964), *Political Adventure*, London

Kunz, Diane (1991), *The Economic Diplomacy of the Suez Crisis*, Chapel Hill, North Carolina

Kyle, Keith (1991), *Suez*, London

Lacouture, Jean (1972) (translated by Daniel Hofstadter), *Nasser*, London

Lamb, Richard (1987), *The Failure of the Eden Government*, London

Little, Douglas (1990), 'Cold War and Covert Action: The United States and Syria, 1945–58', *Middle East Journal* (Winter 1990)

Lloyd, Selwyn (1978), *Suez 1956*, New York

Louis, William Roger (1984), *The British Empire in the Middle East, 1945–51*, Oxford

Louis, William Roger and Owen, Roger (1989), *Suez 1956: The Crisis and its Consequences*, Oxford

Love, Kennett (1970), *Suez: The Twice-Fought War*, London

Lucas, W. Scott (1990), 'The Path to Suez: Britain and the Struggle for the Middle East, 1953–6' in Anne Deighton (ed.), *Britain and the First Cold War*, London

Lucas, W. Scott (1991, to be reprinted in 1996), *Divided We Stand: Britain, the US and the Suez Crisis*, London

Lyon, Peter (1974), *Eisenhower: Portrait of a Hero*, Boston

MacDermott, Geoffrey (1969), *The Eden Legacy*, London

MacDonald, Iveragh (1976), *A Man of the Times*, London

Macmillan, Harold (1971), *Riding the Storm, 1956–9*, London

Bibliography

Massu, Jacques (1978), *Vérité sur Suez*, Paris

Meir, Golda (1975), *My Life*, London

Menzies, Robert (1967), *Afternoon Light*, London

Monroe, Elizabeth (1981), *Britain's Moment in the Middle East, 1914–71*, London

Mosley, Leonard (1978), *Dulles*, New York

Murphy, Robert (1964), *Diplomat Among Warriors*, London

Neff, Donald (1981), *Warriors at Suez*, New York

Neustadt, Richard (1970), *Alliance Politics*, New York

Nutting, Anthony (1967), *No End of a Lesson*, London

Nutting, Anthony (1972), *Nasser*, London

Oren, Michael (1990), 'Secret Egyptian–Israeli Peace Initiatives Prior to the Suez Campaign', *Middle East Journal* (July 1990)

Parmet, Herbert (1972), *Eisenhower and the American Crusade*, London

Partner, Peter (1988), *Arab Voices: The BBC Arabic Service, 1938–88*, London

Pearson, Lester (1974), *Memoirs, Volume II, 1948–57: The International Years*, London

Pincher, Chapman (1978), *Inside Story*, London

Pineau, Christian (1978), *Suez 1956*, Paris

Raphael, Gideon (1981), *Destination Peace: Three Decades of Israeli Foreign Policy*, London

Rhodes James, Robert (1986), *Anthony Eden*, London

Robertson, Terence (1965), *Crisis: The Inside Story of the Suez Crisis*, London

Rothwell, Victor (1992), *Anthony Eden: A Political Biography*, Manchester

Sampson, Anthony (1967), *Macmillan: A Study in Ambiguity*, London

Sayed-Ahmed, Muhammed Abd el-Wahab (1989), *Nasser and American Foreign Policy, 1952–1956*, London

Sharon, Ariel (1989), *Warrior: An Autobiography*, London

Sheffy, Yigal (1990), 'Unconcern at Dawn, Surprise at Sunset: Egyptian Intelligence Appreciations before the Sinai Campaign, 1956', *Intelligence and National Security* (July 1990)

Shlaim, Avi (1983), 'Conflicting Approaches to Israel's Relations with the Arabs: Ben-Gurion and Sharett, 1953–6', *Middle East Journal* (Spring 1983)

Shuckburgh, Evelyn (1986), *Descent to Suez*, London

Thomas, Abel (1978), *Comment Israël fut sauvé*, Paris

Thomas, Hugh (1966), *The Suez Affair*, London

Thompson, Alan (1971), *The Day Before Yesterday*, London

Thorpe, D. R. (1989), *Selwyn Lloyd*, London

Trevelyan, Humphrey (1970), *The Middle East in Revolution*, London

Troen, Selwyn Ilan and Shemesh, Moshe (eds) (1990), *The Suez–Sinai Crisis of 1956: Retrospective and Reappraisal*, London

Verrier, Anthony (1983), *Through the Looking Glass: British Foreign Policy in an Age of Illusions*, London

West, Nigel (1988), *The Friends: Britain's Post-War Secret Intelligence Operations*, London

Williams, Philip (ed.) (1983), *The Diary of Hugh Gaitskell, 1945–56*, London

Wright, Peter (1987), *Spycatcher*, New York

Index

Aldrich, Winthrop, 88, 109
ALPHA, Operation, 10, 14, 15,
   20, 29
Amery, Julian, 59
Anderson mission (1956), 20, 23,
   28
Attlee Government (1945–51), 8

Baghdad Pact, 11–12
   and Egypt, 14
   and US accession, 23, 24, 29–30,
      40
Ben-Gurion, David, 12, 65, 77–9,
   83–4, 89
Britain
   and Egypt
      history, 7
      negotiations over Suez Canal
         Base, 9
   and Iraqi-Jordanian axis, 22, 27,
      77
   and Suez Crisis
      Cabinet meetings, 49, 58–9,
         84–7
      estimate of legal position, 49
      press reaction, 40–1, 53, 70
      relations with France, 69,
         75–6, 83
      relations with Israel, 39, 54,
         65, 70, 83–4

   relations with Soviet Union,
      103–4
   military position in the Middle
      East, 47
   policy in the Middle East, 7–8,
      27–8, 114–16
   relations with US, 8–10
Butler, R.A., 26, 34, 57–8
   plot to remove Eden and,
      109–11

Churchill, Winston, 9, 33, 40, 99
CIA, 10, 16, 29, 38–9, 97, 99

Dayan, Moshe, 12, 78
Dixon, Pierson, 90
Dulles, John Foster, 15, 18–19,
   29–31, 39–44, 62–70, 90,
   92, 98, 106
   and Eden, 35, 51–52
   and Lloyd, 40, 51–2
   and Macmillan, 20–1, 67–8,
      111
   and Nasser, 23, 28, 51–2
   hospitalisation of (November
      1956), 99
   meeting with Lloyd (November
      1956), 108
   meeting with Lloyd and Pineau
      (October 1956), 71

136

.